the child who never was

LOOKING FOR TEGAN LANE

the child who never was

~~LOOKING FOR TEGAN LANE~~

BY ALLISON LANGDON

PARK
STREET
PRESS

Published by Park Street Press
a division of ACP Magazines Ltd (ABN 18 053 273 546)
and Media 21 Publishing Pty Ltd (ABN 82 090 635 073)

ACP Magazines Ltd
54 Park Street, Sydney, GPO Box 4088, Sydney, NSW 1028

Media21 Publishing Pty Ltd
30 Bay Street, Double Bay, NSW 2028
Tel: (02) 9362 1800 Fax: (02) 9362 9500
Email: m21@media21.com.au
Website: www.media21publishing.com

National Library of Australia Cataloguing-in-Publication entry

Langdon, Allison.
 The child who never was : looking for Tegan Lane.

ISBN 9781876624569 (pbk.).

1. Lane, Tegan.
2. Criminal investigation - New South Wales - Sydney.
3. Missing children - New South Wales - Sydney.
4. Newborn infants - Crimes against - New South Wales - Sydney.
5. Victims of crimes - New South Wales - Sydney.
6. Absence and presumption of death - New South Wales - Sydney. I. Title.

364.155092

Design: Buzzard Wings Pty Ltd
Front cover design: Anita Belia, Buzzard Wings Pty Ltd
Cover image: Getty Images
Images: Newspix and courtesy Nine Network
Editor: Katie Ekberg
Colour reproduction: Clayton Lloyd, Flawless Imaging
Printed by: McPhersons Printing Group
Sales: Stephen Balme Email: stephen@media21.com.au

CONTENTS

FOREWORD   9

Chapter 1   **THE HOSPITAL**   11
               The birth of Tegan Lee Lane

Chapter 2   **THE SHOCKING DISCOVERY**   27
               One and one makes three

Chapter 3   **THE INVESTIGATION**   45
               Broken promises and false confessions

Chapter 4   **SO WHO IS KELI LANE?**   65
               Olympic dreams and baby number four

Chapter 5   **THE GRILLING OF DUNCAN GILLIES**   81
               An intimate affair

Chapter 6   **A RESPECTED FAMILY**   99
               Silence, secrets and sadness

Chapter 7   **TEAM PLAYERS**   117
               Family and friends close ranks

Chapter 8   **WHO AND WHERE IS ANDREW NORRIS?**   137
               The invisible man

Chapter 9   **THE SEARCH FOR TEGAN**   155
               A near miss and a dead end

Chapter 10   **KELI TAKES THE STAND**   173
               Will the truth come out?

Chapter 11   **A FRUSTRATED CORONER**   191
               The search must go on

POSTSCRIPT   207

ACKNOWLEDGEMENTS

A VERY WARM thank you to my editor Katie Ekberg for all her help and guidance as I set out to write my first book. I benefited enormously from Katie's many helpful and perceptive suggestions. From the moment this story hit the headlines I found it intriguing and it was with the support of good friend Adam Walters and Norm Lipson that I had the opportunity to do more than cover the story for *National Nine News* and could immerse myself in the challenging task of trying to understand Keli Lane and the decisions she made. For their generous and unwavering support a big thank you! Also thanks to the staff at Westmead Coroner's Court who provided a room and countless transcripts and the New South Wales Police Media Unit for updates with the current police investigation.

To the publishers at Media 21, Stephen, Phil and Craig, thank you for your enthusiasm, countless suggestions and the opportunity to tell this story, which affected me so greatly.

To my partner Mike and my family for their support, love and patience and finally I would like to dedicate this book to Debbie Kiehne (7 April 1970 – 21 November 2006) who always inspired me.

ABOUT THE AUTHOR

ALLISON LANGDON is a respected journalist with the Nine Network. Since joining the *Nightline* program in 2001 she has worked across several different news rounds with acclaim. In 2003 she travelled to China and East Timor covering stories for news and the *Sunday* program. Allison was also one of the first Australian journalists on the ground following the bombing of the Australian Embassy in Jakarta in September 2004. She filed daily for all of Nine's bulletins before following the Australian survivor, five-year-old Manny Musu, to Singapore. In October 2004 she returned to Sydney as a general reporter with *National Nine News* where she excelled covering the court round, including the coronial inquest into the disappearance of Tegan Lane. In early 2007 she joined the *TODAY Show* as newsreader. Allison lives in Sydney.

FOREWORD

KELI LANE is clearly a liar and a practised schemer, but even so she has shouldered an enormous burden. Those who know her best are adamant that she is not a killer but to others it is a very real possibility.

Not since the Lindy Chamberlain mystery has a mother in Australia been so maligned by the public, but at least with baby Azaria, there was a final conclusion. When Lindy Chamberlain reported that her two-month-old daughter Azaria had been snatched from their tent at Uluru in 1980, the "dingo baby" story captured headlines around the world. Azaria's body was never found either, but when her jumpsuit was discovered together with blood in the family car, Lindy was jailed. Later she would be acquitted on new evidence. Sadly in the case of missing baby Tegan Lee Lane, things have worked out differently.

Baby Tegan was born on September 12, 1996 at Auburn Hospital and disappeared two days later into thin air. It is a mystifying case that has gripped the nation.

The reason I wrote this story is because the matter ended up before NSW State Coroner John Abernethy in 2005 when I was then the court reporter for *National Nine News*. I covered the story and was enthralled. The coronial inquest into the suspected death of Tegan Lane came about because police had pretty much come to a dead end with their investigation. Keli had initially cooperated with detectives but stopped talking on the advice of her lawyer.

The Coroner's job was to determine whether or not Tegan was alive or dead, and if deceased, whether anyone could be found responsible for her death and should face possible charges.

From the moment this story hit the headlines it has intrigued me – secret pregnancies, affairs and a newborn baby who simply vanished.

For Coroner Abernethy it would prove to be a frustration. One of his last cases before retiring, it would be the one that bothered him the most, more than any other in his career. He desperately wanted to find out the truth behind the web of lies spun by Keli Lane. He, like the journalists who covered the inquest, probably has an idea as to what he believes happened to Tegan, but it's likely no one other than her mother Keli Lane, will ever know for sure.

There are a number of persons mentioned in the book who cannot be named for legal reasons. In some cases it is because that person is a child and the court's foremost obligation is to protect their identity, and in other cases because they are an adult, who, if identified, would in turn identify a child.

As much as we all speculated throughout the inquest, talking amongst ourselves – the journalists, the police officers, the courtroom staff, the witnesses - the only person who can answer the big question 'Where is baby Tegan?' won't say.

Or perhaps she no longer knows.

Allison Langdon
Sydney 2007

the h●spital
THE BIRTH OF TEGAN LEE LANE

chapter **1**

ON THE AFTERNOON of September 11, 1996, 21-year-old Keli Lane walked into Auburn Hospital in Sydney's west. She was all alone and more crucially, she was nine months pregnant. Having reached her full term Keli had realised she needed an induction and she must have cut a sad and anxious figure as, clutching her pregnant belly, with no one's arm to clasp, she bravely turned up at the remote suburban hospital asking for help.

Keli Lane and her unborn daughter would walk past the weeds growing up from the cracks in the brick pillars of the hospital's front entrance, to the doorstep of Auburn Hospital as one. Three days later, no one would see them leave together, possibly one of the last times mother and daughter would ever see each other again.

Many secrets and many lies later, the story of Keli Lane and her "missing baby" Tegan has become one of Australia's biggest unsolved crimes. Since those traumatic days in hospital, baby Tegan has disappeared without a trace and as Keli Lane's bizarre and upsetting story unfolds, it is hard not to contemplate the very real possibility that Tegan is not just missing, she's dead.

The western suburb of Auburn is about as far removed from Keli's comfortable middle class upbringing on Sydney's northern beaches, as inner city wasteland is to country club golf course. The suburb itself is the fastest growing Muslim community of Sydney, populated by the thousands of Iraqi people who fled the brutal regime of Saddam Hussein. Here English is the second language in a former bastion of true blue Aussie battlers.

The hospital is run down – a far cry from the modern facilities of a private north shore hospital, where one might have expected a young girl of Keli Lane's social status to give birth to her baby. The daughter of a respected retired senior police officer, Keli was raised a Christian in the comfortable suburb of Fairlight, which neighbours the famous beaches of Manly in New South Wales, and was a gregarious and well-liked member of the local community.

It is difficult to imagine how Keli, a promising water-polo player and student at The Australian College of Physical Education at Homebush, would have felt on this unusually sunny September day. She was about to give birth, a moment the other young mums on the maternity ward would cherish as the most important in their life. Was she frightened? Did she have all the same fears; share the same excitement of a mother-to-be? Had she bonded with her unborn child? Did she know its sex? Had she picked a name?

There are so many questions about that day, many of which may never be answered. Questions people can only speculate about. How did a popular, fun-loving girl, from a close-knit family end up in this place: utterly alone, on "the other side of the tracks"? Didn't she have someone she could turn to? Surely she could have confided in her mother, one of her many girlfriends, or even the baby's father?

Instead, blond-haired, tanned, stocky, athletic Keli – who had incredibly concealed her pregnancy with a wardrobe of baggy tracksuits – was alone and almost certainly troubled as she checked herself into Auburn Hospital on September 11, 1996. Keli, who rarely bothered with make-up and liked to wear her medium-length blond hair down, looked large all over as opposed to the usual protruding pregnant belly – later people would remember that she carried the baby more "widthways".

Nurse Susan Jane Cashman can cast her mind back to that day. She was working that particular Wednesday and remembers a young, frightened girl coming in for a CTG (cardiotocography) – a procedure that monitors the baby's heartbeat and contractions – necessary in Keli's case because her baby was overdue.

When Nurse Cashman was called to give evidence at the 2005 coronial inquest into the disappearance of baby Tegan, she said she had thought it unusual that Keli was alone, and recalled her mentioning something about her partner being away playing rugby.

Keli had revealed to Nurse Cashman that she had been planning to have her baby at home with an independent midwife present, but that could no longer happen as she had reached nine months. She was upset that instead of a home birth, she was now at Auburn Hospital for an induction.

A curious Nurse Cashman had wondered why the midwife was not with her, or why she had at least not sent Keli's records along with her – home midwives are extremely diligent and would keep extensive records on their patients. Keli had told hospital staff that her midwife was a woman by the name of Julie Melville, and had given them a phone number to contact "midwife" Melville on.

It was another nurse, Jebunisa Lalani, who was put in charge of tracking down Julie Melville. She was told to do it quickly, as it was important the hospital gained access to Keli's antenatal test results – which would reveal any genetic or congenital abnormalities. Nurse Lalani made several attempts to reach the midwife on the telephone number Keli supplied, but without luck. Auburn Hospital would have to conduct the tests again itself.

Later professionals would discover that incredibly, Keli had driven from another hospital that morning – Ryde Hospital, where she had also undergone tests – before making the decision to turn up on the front doorstep of Auburn Hospital, her chosen place to give birth. At full term, possibly in a certain amount of pain and certainly panicking, Keli still had the wisdom to take herself to a hospital as far away from where she lived as she could manage in her condition; no one she knew must see her, recognise her or know that this baby was about to be born. She would conceal its birth as efficiently as she had concealed her pregnancy.

At Auburn the tests were completed and the decision was made to induce labour overnight on September 11. It wasn't long before contractions began and 21-year-old Keli braced herself to give birth alone. There was no loving partner to squeeze Keli's hand or stroke her forehead when the pain became unbearable, no familiar face looking in her eyes and reassuring her that she was nearly there, doing a marvellous job, that everything would be fine. No one to even hurl abuse at as they told her to push just one more time! But most tragically, no one to share the joy when the doctor told her she'd just given birth to a healthy, happy, beautiful baby girl.

And for Keli, it was by no means an easy birth. When the contractions became unbearable she was given an epidural anaesthesia for pain relief, and according to medical notes "the placenta was retained, requiring manual removal". As a consequence she suffered heavy blood loss of about 1000 millilitres. "Everyone is different," Nurse Cashman told the inquest. "If the lady had previously had surgery and had some scarring, her placenta can attach a little bit more firmly and they don't come away so easily."

When the placenta was removed – an invasive and uncomfortable procedure for Keli – it was found to be calcified. (Placenta calcification refers to calcium deposits, which appear on the placenta; they indicate an aging of the placenta, which occurs near the end of pregnancy.) Nurse Cashman explained to the inquest that placentas become calcified for a number of reasons: "It may be that the pregnancy is overdue, she may have been a smoker." (Keli wasn't a smoker.) She also said that placenta calcification can happen to women who have had previous pregnancies, where scarring occurred – although that was not considered in Keli's case, because she had told hospital staff that it was her first baby.

The delivery of Keli's baby girl was in the capable hands of obstetrician Dr Gregory John Jenkins, who revealed during the inquest that according to his notes at the time there had been several complications with the birth.

"The initial presentation would have been to the delivery suite because Ms Lane wasn't booked in at Auburn Hospital," he explained. "So she would have originally presented to the birthing suite for assessment. We proceeded to an induction of labour thereafter. She would have remained in the birthing suite until after the delivery and

The midwives who helped deliver Tegan would years later remember the newborn and her young vulnerable mother. What sprang to mind was the lack of visitors.

the issue with the placenta was resolved and we were happy that her clinical condition was stable. Then she would have been transferred to the maternity ward or the post-natal ward."

Keli was one of four mums who would give birth at Auburn Hospital that sunny September day in 1996. Two girls and two boys were welcomed into the world, but tragically the other little girl was stillborn. While the devastating loss began to bear down on the distraught parents of the stillborn girl, Keli Lane named her daughter Tegan Lee Lane. While the bereaved family were trying to come to terms with the unthinkable, Keli Lane was thinking their unthinkable: she was not going to keep her baby girl. By a cruel twist of irony, one set of loving parents was left empty-handed, another single mum was left hands full, but not for long.

The midwives who helped deliver Tegan would – when questioned by police years later – remember the newborn well and her young vulnerable mother. Despite having delivered thousands of babies in the three years since Tegan's birth, their vague memories were soon jolted after checking birth records from the time. What sprang immediately to their minds was the lack of visitors. Keli didn't have the usual steady stream of family and friends or a room overflowing with flowers and cards.

Loretta Allen was working the late shift the night of September 12, the day Keli gave birth in the early hours. She arrived at work shortly before nine o'clock in the evening, did a quick check of her patients and did not leave the hospital until after 7am the next morning. According to her notes Nurse Allen popped in to see Keli and her baby several times. Having worked at the hospital since 1993, Loretta Allen remarked that it was rare – especially in an area such as Auburn – for a patient with a newborn to be alone, and not surrounded by family and friends. "At Auburn Hospital, I would find it very unusual that they didn't have visitors," she said.

She had just undergone a physically difficult and traumatic birth, but Keli, who was very fit and strong, seemed to be coping and recovering well. What concerned the nursing staff more than her physical state, though, was lone Keli's emotional well-being and total lack of visitors. Whenever they pressed her about the baby's father, she would become edgy and was evasive. Finally, feeling this patient needed help, they contacted the hospital's social worker.

Social worker Alicia Baltra-Vasquez came to speak to Keli on September 13, the day after Tegan's birth. "I remember she was breastfeeding the baby at the time – she looked quite happy with the baby and she started to talk about many things: her mother, her family and also talked to me about her future, things like that," she said. "She was worried, crying a lot, which is normal because women, when they have a baby, they have a problem with their hormones, so you can easily have blue days, you know, they can cry," she explained to the coronial inquest.

Alicia Baltra-Vasquez took extensive notes on her patient's physical and mental state.

She calmly explained to Keli that her emotions were normal and also to be expected. She wrote in her file that "the client did not expect to have complications post delivery like removal of placenta or haemorrhage." Possibly it was this that was contributing to Keli's distress.

Ms Baltra-Vasquez believed Keli required professional support because she had no partner or parent with her during the delivery or in those critical days directly after the birth.

Physically – considering what she'd been through – Keli, who was of a robust physical stature and about 163cm (5ft 6in) tall, was doing well. She was happy to breastfeed her baby and she wasn't having any problems connecting with her. However the experienced social worker still felt that Keli was going through a painful bereavement process.

What Ms Baltra-Vasquez didn't know as she sat with the tearful young mum, was that she would be one of the last people to see mother and daughter together. Her minutes of calm, trying to reassure Keli, watching her nurse her newborn baby girl Tegan, would literally be the calm before the storm: within a few years this solitary, secretive, enigmatic young woman – who at the time didn't seem out of the ordinary or particularly special – would rocket to infamy in headlines around the world, in a way that only the Lindy and Azaria Chamberlain mystery could match.

(When Lindy Chamberlain reported that her two-month-old daughter Azaria had been snatched from their tent at Uluru in 1980, the "dingo baby" story would capture media headlines across the country. Despite a massive search, Azaria's body was never found, but when her jumpsuit and what appeared to be blood in the Chamberlains' car was discovered, Lindy was sentenced to life for murder. She was later acquitted on the discovery of new evidence.)

But the Keli Lane back in 1996 gave no hint to those around her of what was to come. At no stage did Keli indicate that she did not want to keep her child, or that she had plans to give Tegan away. Again one can only wonder about the thoughts that must have been racing through her mind all those years ago. Was it that the seemingly private patient was secretly in turmoil and thought she had no other option than to give up her baby? Or perhaps she simply didn't feel the instant bond that mothers speak of. Later the inquest would learn about the religious values upheld by Keli's family: was it that she knew abortion was never going to be an option, and in her own confused mind, she was doing the right thing?

At the coronial inquest Alicia Baltra-Vasquez was questioned by Keli's lawyer Peter Hamill.

Mr Hamill: "If Keli was thinking about lawfully adopting out this child, Tegan Lane, and she mentioned that to you, would that be something that you would record in your notes?"

Ms Baltra-Vasquez: "Of course, straight away and immediately I would get all the relevant information [or] we wouldn't discharge the person home!"

But how could the social worker who had innocently witnessed possibly the last moments between Tegan Lane and her mother, know that she could have changed the whole pattern of events, maybe even saved a life, if she had been armed with the facts?

Sadly as the years have since unfolded, it has become evident that hiding the facts was an integral part of Keli's double life. She had already told the social worker a web of lies. She claimed she was born and raised in Perth, where she said her family still lived. She said that she had moved out of the family home when she was 18 years old to live with her boyfriend. She told Ms Baltra-Vasquez that while she was on very good terms with her parents, she quite often clashed with her mother and that their relationship could be tense because they had very different values. She described her boyfriend as "a very caring, good man", said the pregnancy was planned and that they had moved to Sydney a few months prior to the birth, because of his rugby union career.

Determined not to raise suspicions as to why her boyfriend was not with her at the hospital, Keli had also emotionally explained how they had planned to have the baby delivered at home on August 30 – 13 days before Tegan was born. She said her partner wanted to be present for the birth, but things didn't go to plan, as he had to travel overseas in early September to play rugby union.

While Ms Baltra-Vasquez wrote down everything that Keli told her, she also made notes about her own feelings surrounding the breakdown of Keli's support system, which had led her to being alone at such an emotional time. From a professional point of view Keli gave all the signs of being happy with her baby girl – she certainly had no trouble bonding with Tegan – but it was also clear that Keli was in an extremely fragile mental state and this concerned the social worker.

"During the interview Keli had tearful episodes, she said she didn't know why they happened. I told her that it was normal and [I explained to her] why the episodes happen. I [told] her that it was normal and that it's good to express her feelings. Keli recognised that she did have great expectations about the birth of her child."

Despite the occasional breakdown in front of the kindly social worker, perhaps hinting at her patient's real feelings, Keli stuck firmly to her guns and remained adamant that she wanted to be discharged from hospital on Saturday September 14 – just two days after the problematic birth. It seemed an overly-ambitious goal: a young mum, who required post-operative care and who appeared to be emotionally needy, expecting to cope alone at home with her newborn, after spending such little time in hospital. But Keli was insistent. "Keli stated that she is fit to be discharged, and [that] she will manage well at home," recorded Ms Baltra-Vasquez in the handwritten notes she made at the time.

Under Auburn Hospital's domiciliary midwifery program, mothers could be discharged as early as six hours after the birth. The program was set up especially for mothers who had a trouble-free delivery, and who had plenty of help waiting at home. The program also benefits the hospital by clearing beds quickly for the next round of mums-to-be. Once home, the new mums are visited by a midwife for up to seven days after delivery. During the daily home visits the midwife would check all of the baby's vitals, such as temperature, bowel movements and that they were feeding properly. They would also conduct a quick medical examination of the mother. At Auburn Hospital Karen Lisa Johns was in charge of the program when Tegan was born. "Any questions the mother might have about mothering skills – they can call us at any time if they have a problem," she explained at the inquest. "So we just go to them rather than leave them in the hospital if they're self-sufficient."

WHEN TOLD it was doubtful she would be considered a suitable candidate for the early release program, Keli was quick to come up with a solid back-up story. She claimed that she had a lady coming to the house to stay with her until her parents arrived from Perth on the Tuesday (although she was quite vague as to who that person would be), plus, she said that her boyfriend would be back in Australia on the Wednesday, and her own midwife Julie Melville would make regular home visits to ensure she was coping well. To the social worker it now appeared Keli would have a good network of support once she got home – her family would be arriving in Sydney three days after Keli arrived home, and her partner would return from his sporting trip the day after.

One of the last notes Ms Baltra-Vasquez would make was about Keli's partner, the rugby player Keli told her was Tegan's father. Keli had gone on to assure the concerned social worker that within three months she, her boyfriend and their baby daughter would be leaving Australia for London, where they'd live for a couple of years as her partner pursued his rugby career. His name, she finally revealed was Duncan Gillies.

It was Stephen Keith Chen – a medical officer in Auburn's emergency ward – who was asked to medically review baby Tegan and her mother one last time before they were discharged. According to his medical notes he was contacted by nursery staff at 2pm on September 14 to conduct a thorough head-to-toe examination of the child. He ruled baby Tegan and her mother were fit to go home.

But the nurse in charge of the domiciliary midwifery program, Karen Lisa Johns, was still suspicious about Keli's early release – she thought it was odd that Keli wanted to be discharged into the care of a homebirth midwife who no one at the hospital had ever met. And she added at the inquest, "In my experience homebirth midwives are very possessive of their patients and they [tend to be] very disappointed when they have to come to the hospital [so their patient can] be induced, and they would be with them and they would be a support person present during the birth."

Not once had Ms Melville called the hospital to check on her patient, nor had she stopped in to visit. "I just thought why wouldn't the midwife ring and just sort of organise that with me?" said Ms Johns. "As a midwife myself I would never leave that to the patient. I couldn't really understand why the midwife wouldn't have called and done that herself, especially if we were checking her haemoglobin."

Sadly the mystification over the midwife was the last alarm bell to ring, just as it had been the first – when Keli had just arrived at the hospital, Nurse Susan Jane Cashman, just like her colleague Karen Lisa Johns, was curious as to why Keli's midwife was not with her, or at the very least had not sent her medical files.

What the hospital staff didn't know was that Julie Melville was boyfriend Duncan Gillies mother, which would also mean – if indeed Duncan was the father – she was Tegan's grandmother. But Julie Melville, a registered nurse, was not aware of the pregnancy. Keli had provided the nurses with a false phone number, which is why Nurse Jebunisa Lalani had been unable to contact Keli's "midwife."

When police finally made contact with Ms Melville in 1999 she was shocked to learn that Keli had given birth, and she flatly denied having ever acted as her midwife. "I was never aware that Keli Lane had given birth to any child," she said. She was adamant she had never spoken to Keli about the pregnancy and had not – at any stage during or after the birth – provided any counselling or midwifery services.

The vital question about her midwife was raised with Keli when she took part in her first recorded police interview on February 14, 2001 – Valentine's Day – at Manly police station. Detective Senior Constable Mathew James Kehoe and Senior Constable Glen MacKillop asked her why she had listed Julie Melville as the midwife.

Det. Sen. Con. Kehoe: "You were referred to the hospital by a home birth midwife. Is that correct?"

Ms Lane: "No, it's not correct."

Det. Sen. Con. Kehoe: "All right. Can you tell me who Julie Melville is?"

Ms Lane: "Yeah, Julie was the mother of the guy I was seeing at the time, who was a midwife."

Det. Sen. Con. Kehoe: "Oh, okay. And you just supplied her name. Is that correct?"

Ms Lane: "That's right. If they needed to reach someone or I needed some support then I wanted her to be contacted."

Det. Sen. Con. Kehoe: "Oh, right okay. To your knowledge, do you know if she was ever contacted?"

Ms Lane: "I don't know."

Of course Julie Melville was never contacted – there was no way Keli could have Duncan's mother find out about the baby, as her son Duncan didn't know about the pregnancy either. Why? Because, as Keli later revealed, he wasn't the father!

Keli was about to change her story and it wouldn't be the first time. When the nurses were called to give evidence at the inquest they were pretty sure she didn't have any visitors. But Keli was about to claim to police that she did have a visitor and a very important one at that. Now she claimed the baby's natural father, a man by the name of Andrew Morris with whom she had a brief affair, had visited her at Auburn Hospital in 1996.

"After a brief affair with the father of the child, I gave birth," Keli told police. "We made an arrangement that he would come and take

For the first time police learnt something about the baby's natural father ... Keli claimed he was a man by the name of Andrew Morris with whom she'd had a brief affair.

custody of Tegan as I was unable to take care of her myself. And he dropped me home and then took Tegan with him into his care."

Keli said that the man she now claimed to be Tegan's father, Andrew Morris, came to see her on only two occasions. The first visit was the day after Tegan was born when he arrived in the evening some time after 5pm. He was not alone though; he had with him his long-term partner Mel and his mother. According to Keli, the visitors did not stay long – just enough time to discuss his taking custody of Tegan and to talk about buying a baby seat. "He was to arrange to have a car seat organised," said Keli. "So he could take Tegan home. He was to take me home, and then he would go home with Tegan."

But still no one who worked at the hospital remembered seeing any visitors in Keli's room. Equally it was so long ago, they could not rule it out.

What midwife Ann Marie Hanlon did remember though, was Keli's request to be discharged from hospital just two days after the birth. "When I wrote the day's discharge report at two o'clock (pm)," she confirmed to police "the room was empty, the bed was empty, the cot was empty and all her personal belongings had gone."

She did not see Keli and Tegan leave the hospital, so she couldn't be sure if they had done so alone, or accompanied by family or friends. If Nurse Hanlon had been present at the time, she would certainly have recorded it in her notes. For police it was incredibly frustrating to know that had someone seen Keli leave the hospital, they might have been able to shed some light on what happened next in the car park. But no one had.

In the final critical minutes before she left Auburn Hospital, Keli was asked to fill in baby Tegan's registration form. It was handed to her by a ward clerk in a blue folder and contained both the social security and the registration form, and also an application to add Tegan to her Medicare card. "When I filled out the registration forms in the hospital," Keli said, "I went through them with a nurse and she had the official sticker or whatever it is. I filled out the registration forms and signed them, and also signed a form for Medicare in case Tegan was with me in the future and I needed to take her to the doctor's or something."

Then with the papers signed, Keli packed her belongings, bundled Tegan into her arms and walked out of Auburn Hospital – it was some time around 2pm, although the hospital notes regarding the time she was discharged are slightly contradictory. According to Dr Chen, he examined the pair at 2pm, while Nurse Hanlon had already noted the room being empty at that time. Keli too was a little hazy about the exact time, but believed it was a little earlier when police questioned her five years later

Det. Sen. Con. Kehoe: "You remained in hospital until the …"

Ms Lane: "Saturday."

Det. Sen. Con. Kehoe: "… the 16th of September."

Ms Lane: "I'm not sure of the date … but I know that it was a Saturday."

Det. Sen. Con. Kehoe: "That would have been the 14th of September, sorry. Do you recall what time you would have left hospital?"

Ms Lane: "It would have been before 12 o'clock sometime."

Keli said she made her way across the hospital car park to where Andrew Morris was waiting with his mother and girlfriend.

Det. Sen. Con. Kehoe: "On the day you were discharged from hospital Andrew came to the hospital. Is that right?"

Ms Lane: "That's correct."

Det. Sen. Con. Kehoe: "And they dropped you to….They dropped you home to Gladesville?"

Ms Lane: "That's right."

Det. Sen. Con. Kehoe: "And what address did they drop you to in Gladesville?"

Ms Lane: "10 Venus Street, Gladesville."

Det. Sen. Con. Kehoe: "And Andrew took Tegan home with him?"

Ms Lane: "That's right."

JUST AN HOUR later Keli rushed into her parents' home at Fairlight, (where she still lived most of the time, when not sleeping over at her boyfriend Duncan's house), on the other side of Sydney, to be greeted by her mother and Duncan Gillies, who were sitting at the kitchen table enjoying a coffee together. She was running late. She was expected at a friend's wedding in Manly with Duncan in less than an hour. Hurriedly she changed into a smart cream Country Road skirt and jacket suit and the pair raced out of the door, arriving at the church just before 4pm.

As they took their seats in a pew, surrounded by family and friends, not one single person in that church – other than Keli – had any inkling of what a traumatic event had just taken place. Not one person noticed that anything was amiss with the golden-haired water-polo champ Keli Lane. Indeed she looked as full of life as ever. Her friends and family had no idea about her pregnancy and at that point it must have seemed to Keli that they never would.

As she watched her friends Craig and Dianne Hansen tie the knot, one can only imagine what was running through her head. Was she relieved that such a turbulent period in her life was over? Was she silently grieving? Or was she simply happy that she had given birth, offloaded the baby and amazed that she had got away with it?

the shocking discovery

ONE AND ONE MAKES THREE

AS THE WEEKS turned to months and the months turned to years, Keli surely must have thought her secret was now well and truly safe: by 1999 no one knew that three years earlier she had given birth to a baby girl she named Tegan Lee. Gradually she must have fallen back into her old routine; still playing her beloved water-polo and catching up with girlfriends in the pubs around Manly, near to where she lived at her parents' home in Fairlight. By now she was working as a PE teacher at the exclusive Ravenswood School for Girls in Gordon, run by the Uniting Church. As time passed the enormity of what she had done must have faded to a point where any thought of Tegan was fleeting. She felt safe in the knowledge that no one knew her secret, but that was all about to come undone.

Indeed Keli Lane's life was about to be turned upside down, even though it would incredibly be another two years, not until 2001, that a police operation would be mounted. Keli's lies were about to spiral beyond control. Lies that would ultimately drag countless people – friends, family and those in authority – through years of painstaking disbelief and anxiety in their efforts to get to the truth.

It's 1999 and industrious child protection worker John Matthew Borovnik, the district officer of DoCS (the NSW Department of Community Services, which promotes the safety and well-being of children and young people), is busy at his desk in Katoomba in the Blue Mountains (just west of Sydney) when a strange file came across his desk. Initially it appeared to be a straightforward adoption report. The mother was listed as Ms Keli Lane, a 24-year-old woman, who had just given birth to a baby boy at Ryde Hospital on the May 31, 1999. According to the document in front of him, it was her first child.

Staff at Ryde Hospital became concerned for 24-year-old Keli Lane the day after she gave birth to a healthy baby – a boy. They rang social worker Virginia Fung from Anglicare Adoption Services at Telopea, Parramatta, because the mother was showing signs of distress. Keli kept repeating that she was unable to keep the baby and wanted to have him adopted out. Ms Fung organised to come to the hospital to see Keli the following day, June 2.

This was a most unusual course of action. Normally if a mother wanted to adopt out a child she would make contact with the agency during the pregnancy, or rely on her general practitioner to do so on her behalf. Alternatively, the adoption agency would be contacted during the antenatal period at hospital – it was extremely rare for an adoption agency to be called this late, actually after the birth of the baby.

On that first visit Keli told Ms Fung that the father of her child was her boyfriend Duncan Gillies and the reason she could not keep the baby was because she wanted to move to London to live for a short time. To Ms Fung it appeared that Keli had made up her mind. "At the time I think I remember Keli actually saying that adoption is the only option, there's no way she could actually parent a baby," she told the coronial inquest.

Experience told Ms Fung to leave it for a few days before organising another meeting with Keli, so as to give her more time to think about her decision. Ms Fung wanted to get to bottom of what had prompted Keli's decision, as it seemed to be a very rash one and she wanted to talk about what other options were available, other than adoption. "If they [the parents] are still quite insistent that they want to go through with the process then we actually have a voluntary foster care period, where the parents can actually test themselves being physically separated from the baby to see if adoption really is something that they can cope with."

So while Keli was left to ponder her decision, her baby son was put on a short term placement with foster parents in the Blue Mountains. "We need to feel that we have actually explored all the issues with the parent before we actually decide to go through to the next stage which is for the parent to actually sign the adoption consent forms," said Ms Fung. While a parent can sign the adoption papers five days after a birth, it was decided that would be too soon for Keli and it was agreed that she should wait for at least a month. Ms Fung wasn't at all sure at that stage if Keli really wanted to give up her baby, so she wanted to give the scared new mother as much time as possible to reach her final decision.

Five days passed before Keli next met with Ms Fung at the social worker's office at Telopea. "During our conversation I questioned her as to her having previous children. She informed me that this was her first child," said Ms Fung. Later that day Ms Fung contacted Mr Borovnik – who was handling the case for DoCS because the foster parents lived in Katoomba where his office was – to inform him of what was happening with the case. By that stage Mr Borovnik was already making a few inquiries of his own.

Ms Fung still wasn't convinced that Keli really wanted to give up the child and so wanting to be thorough, she wasted no time trying to hunt down Duncan Gillies who was listed as the child's father. Despite being given a wrong telephone number, she finally reached him by way of a letter sent to his rugby club.

Duncan Gillies rang her back shocked! He was adamant that he knew nothing about any child being born and he flatly refuted that he was the father. Still reeling from the conversation, Ms Fung rang Keli on July 28 and told her about the conversation she'd had with Duncan. "He is not the father!" Keli yelped. After a short pause Ms Fung gently suggested that they should meet again at her office.

It was there Keli spun her next story. The father of her baby boy, she now announced to the social worker, was a man by the name of Aaron Williams, an Australian now living in London.

Again, Keli was to impress Ms Fung – as she had impressed Ms Baltra-Vasquez when nursing tiny Tegan three years before - with her handling of her newborn. Keli saw her son three or four times in the months after the birth, always at Ms Fung's office, and, reveals the social worker, she had natural mothering instincts.

"She was very competent," said Ms Fung. "She was very caring and loving when she held him. It was not an easy time, so there were lots of tears as well in terms of her agonising over her decision, whether it was the right decision or not, and she was always very happy to see her son and see how much he had grown and how well he was doing." Over those four months Ms Fung formed a very positive impression of Keli: "I have to say she was a very caring mother."

Between Keli's visits to see her son at Ms Fung's Telopea office, Ms Fung was trying to contact Duncan Gillies again, but was having no luck. She was not certain that she believed his or Keli's denial that he was the father. She suspected that he may know more than he was letting on. She had reached this conclusion after ringing the institution in London where Keli claimed Aaron Williams – the man she now said was the baby boy's father – worked. They had never heard of any such person, and had insisted that he had never worked there.

Ms Fung was not strong enough in her conviction to accuse Mr Gillies of lying; she knew enough about adoption to realise that there is nearly always some degree of secrecy and at the end of the day it was not mandatory that they get to the bottom of who the father was. "Ideally we would like to, for the benefit of the child but I guess in this situation we believe that Keli had told us all that she could and that we had also exhausted our avenues in terms of trying to locate the father."

While Virginia Fung dealt with Keli, Mr Borovnik was looking into the history of her son's birth. Noting that the child was born at Ryde Hospital, he decided that would be his starting point. He rang the hospital and spoke to administration worker Kelly Hennessy to confirm details of the baby's birth. It was during this conversation that Ms Hennessy mentioned in passing that Keli had also been examined at Ryde Hospital nearly three years earlier.

The hospital records showed that Keli had turned up on September 7, 1996 with pain in her upper ribs. Initially doctors believed it was a gall bladder problem but then the innocent administration worker dropped a bombshell. She said that the ultrasound was clear and it was put down to the baby moving. Mr Borovnik was shocked – Keli had not mentioned any previous pregnancies to the adoption agency; in fact she had told Ms Fung that this was her first pregnancy.

Keli left Ryde Hospital but came back four days later on the morning of September 11. That same afternoon she headed straight for Auburn Hospital – strangely a hospital she had never been to before – where she admitted herself. The next day she gave birth to daughter Tegan there. (Keli's hospital choices are shrouded in mystery – neither Ryde nor Auburn was especially close to where she was living, but no explanation for this was given at the inquest.)

Now Mr Borovnik was armed with a crucial piece of evidence: finally a person in a position of authority was aware of the existence of "missing" Tegan Lee Lane. Assuming that Keli would have wanted to adopt out this baby too, he made a call to Alison Smith from the DoCS adoption branch to see if she had any files on this child born in 1996.

Very strict guidelines are in place for adoption in New South Wales,

What the child protection worker was about to hear would haunt him for years to come ... all of a sudden a simple piece of paperwork had become complex and mysterious.

as in all states and territories in Australia. Once a parent signs the adoption consent form, that child is effectively under the care of the Director-General of DoCS until suitable parents are found – and that normally takes about six months. The new parents must be listed on the DoCS Register of Approved Adoptive Applicants, so if Tegan had been adopted out the department would have a record of it. Mr Borovnik expected the adoption branch to have the child's paperwork on file.

But what John Matthew Borovnik was about to hear would haunt him for years to come. "I rang them about Tegan," he told the inquest. "When they rang me back they said 'Are you talking about the baby in 1995?' I said: 'What baby in 1995? I am talking about the baby in 1996!'"

Now Mr Borovnik was well and truly confused. All of a sudden the relatively straightforward process of completing paperwork for the adoption of a baby boy had become very complex and mysterious. It appeared that Keli may have given birth to a third baby, born in 1995, who she'd put up for adoption. Then there was Tegan, born on September 12, 1996, and now her son, born on May 31, 1999, who she also wanted adopted out.

Swiftly Borovnik's department managed to locate files for baby number one – a girl born at the King George V wing of the Royal

Prince Alfred Hospital (RPA), at Camperdown on March 19, 1995, who had been adopted out through the services run by Centacare Catholic Community Services.

But, worryingly, their search for files for baby number two – who we know was Tegan – and her possible adoption proved fruitless. According to their search she didn't exist, and she certainly hadn't been adopted out.

It was social worker Debra Lee Habib who spoke to a 19-year-old Keli in the days after the birth of her first child, a girl – born two days before Keli's 20th birthday in 1995. Mrs Habib remembered Keli wanted to give away the infant because, she said, it would interfere with her dream to represent Australia at the Sydney 2000 Olympic Games in the water-polo.

Mrs Habib believed it wasn't an easy decision for Keli to make since the teenage mother was often tearful when she spoke about her decision. Even so, she was determined that nothing would get in the way of her dream. "She was teary at first, but once we got talking she spoke clearly and appeared to have set goals. She told me she wanted to go to the Sydney 2000 Olympic Games to compete in water-polo," Mrs Habib told the inquest.

"I understood from our conversation that her reason for wanting to put the child up for adoption was that she felt she couldn't achieve her goals if she continued to parent the baby."

Incredibly, Keli's water-polo team mates were later – when Keli's story became public – forced to come to terms with the fact that she was, at one point, swimming competitively alongside them when she was seven months' pregnant and in fact when she excelled at the Junior Pan Am Water Polo World Championships in Quebec in August 1995, she did so shortly after giving birth to baby number one.

The day before her 20th birthday, Keli was granted permission to leave the hospital overnight so she could discuss the option of adoption with the child's father, who she had listed as Duncan Gillies. She left at around 6pm on March 20. While Keli didn't tell Mrs Habib her partner's actual name, she did say that he too wanted to have the baby adopted out because of his rugby commitments. Keli returned to the hospital the following morning, alone. It was her 20th birthday, March 21, 1995. Thoughtful hospital staff brought in a cake to celebrate, but they were the only people to wish her a happy birthday that day – no one else knew where she was. How could they? Where had she told her parents, her brother, her boyfriend, her many school and sporting friends that she would be spending her special day?

When Keli informed staff at RPA that she was certain that she did not want to keep her baby daughter, Centacare worker Angharad Candlin was called in to handle the case. On April 3, 15 days after the birth of the baby girl, Keli signed the consent papers for her baby to be adopted. She had a month's grace to change her mind.

But Keli did not get back in touch and Ms Candlin was worried about the young mother's reaction to the adoption of her daughter. "We were concerned for her because we hadn't heard, you know, we didn't know how she was." Centacare was also having enormous trouble trying to reach Duncan Gillies, who had been listed as the father. "Contacting Duncan was particularly difficult," said Ms Candlin. "We had no reason to suspect that the information that we had was incorrect. So it was unusual because we had all the information, and we still couldn't get him to be involved."

Once the 30-day revocation period ended, Keli's baby girl was placed with its adoptive parents, but it would take a further six to 12 months before the matter would go before the Supreme Court where it would be finalised.

Adoption was a grim process in the past, both for the young mums handing their babies into the arms of strangers and the babies themselves, who, when they grew up, had little chance of tracing their birth mothers. In the 1970s agencies handled around 300 adoptions a year and birth parents had no contact at all with their children once they had signed the papers and handed over their babies. For many children and parents that policy led to years and years of desperate searching for their loved ones, often without a result.

Happily, thanks to fresh new laws all that has changed. Learning from past heartaches, today's birth parents are encouraged to remain active in their child's life. It is even considered in the child's best interests to keep the name given to them by their birth parents – delightfully it is considered a gift.

Adoptions though are rare now and the number has dropped drastically to no more than 20 a year in New South Wales.

But what was really worrying Child Protection Officer John Matthew Borovnik back in 1999, as he sat in his Katoomba office, mulling over the latest piece of information he had unearthed, was what had happened to baby number two, the baby we now know was Tegan Lee Lane. His department had easily located Keli's first baby, a girl, born in 1995 and adopted out – a baby he would never have been made aware of had it not been for a passing comment from a hospital administrator at Ryde Hospital. He was aware of her third baby, a boy, whom Keli was currently requesting be adopted out too. But what on earth had happened to the mystery middle baby, the second baby girl born in 1996? He realised how easy it could have been for the existence of Tegan to have never become known. His department could find no records of her being adopted out. So where was she? She couldn't have just vanished into thin air. At this moment he had no idea what his discovery would lead to, that he was about to open a can of worms.

Slowly and steadily he started his detective work. Still puzzled by what he had uncovered, Mr Borovnik notified his case work manager of his intentions to follow up on this new information. He started with a phone call to Auburn Hospital, where Tegan was born, and requested access to Keli's medical files. It confirmed what he already knew, that the baby girl was born on September 12.

The doctor was asked what she knew about the whereabouts of the other children. She didn't know what to say – it was the first she'd heard of Keli having give birth to others.

Mr Borovnik then called the psychiatrist who had just assessed Keli prior to giving her third child, a son, up for adoption. Mr Borovnik told Dr Debra Montgomery that Keli had given birth to two previous children and that they were trying to trace the whereabouts of the second, a baby girl. The doctor didn't know what to say – it was the first she had heard of Keli having given birth to any other children besides the boy born on May 31.

Dr Montgomery had been asked specifically by Centacare to see Keli Lane to determine whether she was in a sufficiently stable psychiatric state to make an informed decision about the adoption. According to her report, there was no evidence of any psychiatric disturbance that would significantly impair her cognitive capacity or judgment – but then Dr Montgomery made that decision with her hands tied – she did not know about the existence of two other children.

By this time Virginia Fung, the social worker from the adoption agency handling Keli and her son's case, had also been made aware of the existence of the first child (but not Tegan). Borovnik's DoCS colleague Alison Smith – the one who had blown the whistle on Keli's 1995 birth on the telephone to him – had rung Fung on the October 11, 1999 and filled her in.

It was obvious that it was time for another meeting with Keli and this time it took place outside Ravenswood School for Girls, the prestigious day and boarding school where Keli was working as a PE teacher. "I confronted her about the fact that her (baby boy) had a half-sibling," said Ms Fung, who at that stage was still unaware of the birth of Tegan in 1996. Initially a shocked Keli denied giving birth to any other child, but she eventually broke down and cried, admitting to the birth of her first daughter. The following day Keli walked out of the school to find Ms Fung waiting for her again. They waited until the demob-happy pupils had dashed out of the front gates, and once quiet was resumed, tears welled up in Keli's eyes and she confided: "I'm glad that you have found out."

"She was very emotional," explained Ms Fung at the inquest. "She went on to say she had concealed the birth from us because she believed nobody would help her." Sobbing, Keli added that when her parents found out about the first baby, the girl she had at just 19 years old, they had angrily disowned her.

But Keli's tightly-knit web of lies was starting to unravel. As the child protection officer in Katoomba in the Blue Mountains dialled the social worker in Telopea, the full horror of Keli's childbirth history began to dawn in vivid colour on the professionals. When Ms Fung spoke to Mr Borovnik on October 13, less than 24 hours after her last discussion with Keli, he dropped the big bombshell – there was a third child, and no one knew where she was.

Now Mr Borovnik decided that he had to make contact with Keli directly, so he called her at Ravenswood School. Exactly as she had done with Ms Fung over enquiries about her first child, Keli initially denied the existence of baby number two, Tegan, and would not be drawn further. It was at that point Mr Borovnik realised he would have to report the missing child. When he told Keli the police would have to become involved, the conversation ended abruptly.

Four days later a facsimile arrived on Mr Borovnik's desk; it was from Keli, requesting him not to contact any person without giving her prior notice. In that letter she mentioned that neither former boyfriend Duncan Gillies – they split in 1998 – nor Gillies' mother Julie Melville knew about any of the births, and she certainly did not want them to find out through police inquiries. Armed with this information Mr Borovnik rang the local Katoomba police station on November 4 and explained what he had uncovered. He revealed to officers his fears that something sinister may have happened to the child.

The net was beginning to close around Keli Lane.

Keli, realising that her social worker Virginia Fung would soon be put in the picture, now that the DoCS was aware of all three children, decided to write to the woman she had come to know and trust. Wanting to confess, but not being able to summon the courage to do so face to face, she typed a letter and faxed it from Ravenswood School at 10:05am.

October 25, 1999

Dear Virginia,
There were three children, obviously I can't lie anymore, because the paperwork is there, the middle child (Tegan) lives with a family in Perth, although I have not had contact with them for some time, they befriended me just before I had her and supported us. I am not able to give many details, as I am not sure of them myself. If my story is unusual enough, as it already is, I know you probably can't believe it, but I know somehow that you know I am being honest with you..... I am being honest with you.

Even though the matter was now in the hands of the police, Ms Fung continued to write to Keli, although she never saw her again in person. "We did not really talk about Tegan. The only time that she really told me anything about Tegan was in the fax that she sent me." By this stage, perhaps embarrassed, Keli made the decision to cut contact with Ms Fung. "I sent her a couple of letters," said Ms Fung, "and the only response I got back was a message left on my answering machine in March 2000 to say that she's settling in (to her new life without the baby) and things are okay."

Even though Keli was refusing to maintain contact, faithful Ms Fung didn't give up hope, and she continued to forward Keli pictures of her son and letters written by his adoptive parents telling how well he was doing. Sadly, in spite of her efforts, each letter was returned unopened stamped with 'sent to the wrong address'.

Virginia Fung was probably the only professional – probably the only person – who came close to understanding what was going through Keli's mind at this traumatic time. They formed a bond, but in the end, lonely Keli couldn't even confide in her trusted social worker. The bottom line was surely that Keli felt she couldn't tell anyone, not even Ms Fung, the truth about her daughter. Throughout each pregnancy all she did was lie, tell story after story to hospital staff, social workers and the adoption agencies. She denied the existence of Tegan and of her first born daughter because she feared no one would help her adopt out her third child, her son – at least that is what she told Detective Senior Constable Richard Gaut from Manly Police Station when he interviewed her on the May 9, 2003 – four years later.

Det. Sen. Con. Gaut: "Can you tell me why you denied Tegan?"

Ms Lane: "Yeah, because I didn't think they (Anglicare) would help me."

Det. Sen. Con. Gaut: "Right."

Ms Lane: "I thought she'd (Ms Fung) judge me and wouldn't help (my son)…"

Det. Sen. Con. Gaut: "What do you mean, help? Allow you to have the child adopted?"

Ms Lane: "Well, yeah. Or guide me."

But the letter Keli faxed to Virginia Fung in October 1999, explaining that Tegan was living with a family in Perth, was completely different to the story she had told her other social worker, Alicia Baltra-Vasquez at Auburn Hospital, at the time of Tegan's birth in September 1996. She had told Baltra-Vasquez that her partner was playing football overseas, so was unable to be at the birth, and they were looking to move to London as a family to live for a while. In an attempt to determine which, if either of the two stories was correct, Detective Senior Constable Gaut asked Keli about the fax she sent Ms Fung.

Det. Sen. Con. Gaut: "Are the contents of that letter true?"

Ms Lane: "I'm not sure. Some of it, I'm not sure of."

Det. Sen. Con. Gaut: "OK, the middle child, who are you referring to?"

Ms Lane: "That's Tegan."

Det. Sen. Con. Gaut: "Tegan. And you say there the middle child lives with a family in Perth. Is that true?"

Ms Lane: "I'm not sure where they are."

Det. Sen. Con. Gaut: "Well, did you, at the time you wrote this letter, did you believe they were in Perth?"

Ms Lane: "I wasn't sure what Andrew was going to do."

By Andrew, Keli meant Andrew Morris, the man she told police she'd had a brief affair with and was Tegan's father and who visited her in hospital.

But Detective Senior Constable Gaut was sceptical that the couple Keli mentioned in the fax was actually Mr Morris and his partner Mel. Disbelieving her, he continued to press her on it.

Det. Sen. Con. Gaut: "Okay, it says there 'they befriended me just before I had her and supported us.' Is that true?"

Ms Lane: "Well, I got to know Mel a little, I guess. And the support was that they were going to have Tegan, I guess. The support came from knowing she was going to be okay."

Det. Sen. Con. Gaut: "So, are you saying you're referring to Mel and Andrew?"

Ms Lane: "Andrew."

Det. Sen. Con. Gaut: "Well, do you agree that if, if you had an affair with Andrew, who, who knew you well before you had the child …"

Ms Lane: "But I didn't know Mel at all."

THE STORY just didn't seem to add up. Keli claimed the couple she had given Tegan to befriended her shortly before the birth. Yet she was also claiming that man was the child's natural father. They couldn't be one and the same: if the man was Tegan's father he would have to have known Keli for a lot longer; at least nine months!

It wasn't just the police who didn't believe Keli's stories. Further checks by Mr Borovnik and his staff revealed that Keli had given false phone numbers and addresses for all of the three births. The Auburn Hospital records for Tegan stated Keli's address as 70 Venus Street, Gladesville, but that house number didn't exist. It was however the same street in which Duncan Gillies was living at that time, only he was residing at number 10.

Lie just seemed to follow lie. The telephone number Keli had given for her "midwife" Julie Melville – actually then boyfriend Duncan Gillies' mother – must have been false too.

Keli had insisted to perplexed staff at Auburn Hospital it was correct, even though every time the nurses tried it the phone message declared the service was "not in use" and in the end – swamped by their workloads – they simply forgot to follow it up.

Keli named her next of kin as Katie Holt – a close girlfriend – who, when questioned by police, said she knew nothing about the births.

"You've given her name but the number you've given is not her number. Do you recall actually consciously giving the wrong contact numbers so that the hospital wouldn't inadvertently contact those people?" Detective Senior Constable Gaut asked Keli.

Tragically, as the truth about Keli Lane's lies emerged, the people who were in authority realised that countless clues had been missed and mistakes made.

"I would say yes," replied Keli "I probably did because I was protecting myself or others."

Tragically, as the truth about Keli's lies emerged, those in authority realised that countless clues had been missed and mistakes made.

One of the most damaging was the fact that records at Auburn Hospital show Tegan had not submitted a "Guthrie Spot" – a standard procedure where a blood sample is taken from a newborn baby once it is 72 hours old. It's effectively making a note of the child's DNA. The test is taken using blotting paper and sealed in a little yellow envelope – it's a quick way for doctors to check for congenital problems, which if detected can be easily treated.

Keli escaped without Tegan having the test conducted because she discharged herself and her baby just two days after the birth and the staff didn't follow up with the procedure, because they genuinely believed she was now in the care of her own midwife. It was just one of the many checks overlooked, but a crucial one – with no blood sample of Tegan on record, and no idea as to the whereabouts of Tegan herself, it was impossible to discover who her father was.

If there was a consistency in Keli's misinformation it was that all of her hospital records bear Duncan Gillies' name as the father of her three babies. Also consistent: the fact that none of the personal details she gave were correct. At the 2005 inquest Keli's lawyer Peter Hamill jumped on that misinformation, and the fact that it wasn't just Tegan's birth that his client had lied about, but rather all three pregnancies. In all there were more than 10 pieces of misinformation on her forms, from addresses to phone numbers, whereabouts of her parents and identity of the father.

"Do you agree that all of that misinformation in respect of all three children was consistent with a woman who was trying to hide the fact that she had had these babies from everybody in her life?" Hamill asked the detective in charge. "That's correct," replied Detective Senior Constable Gaut.

But mistakes, secrets, lies aside, at the heart of the case was still a missing child. Where was Tegan Lee Lane, who would now be three years old, that is, if she was still alive? There was now a growing fear among police, child protection workers and adoption workers about the child's safety.

There are only four adoption agencies in NSW: the two Keli dealt with – Centacare and Anglicare – as well as DoCS and Barnardo's, which typically dealt with older children rather than newborns. Whenever an adoption is being considered, the parents are clearly informed that private adoption is illegal, and can carry a jail term. "Sometimes in the course of conversation," explained Ms Fung, "they might actually say 'well we know a friend' or something. And that's when we tend to actually raise the point that there could be a difficulty, complications, and actually it's illegal in NSW to arrange private adoptions."

And with Keli's secret now in the hands of the professionals, at this stage none of them could rule out the possibility that Keli Lane may have sold her baby, or even worse, that baby Tegan was no longer alive. But incredibly it would still be several years before Keli Lane's "old routine" way of life would be interrupted.

the investigation
BROKEN PROMISES AND FALSE CONFESSIONS

chapter **3**

FROM THE VERY start the investigation into the disappearance of baby Tegan was going to be difficult. A newborn child vanishes without a trace two days after her birth and no one saw her leave the hospital in the arms of her mother Keli Lane. What happened in the two hours that it took Keli to leave Auburn Hospital at 2 pm on September 14, 1996 and reach the church in Manly on the other side of the city where she would witness her friends' wedding at 4 pm?

Tegan has not been seen or heard of since.

This was a cold case, the hardest to crack, with very few leads and no witnesses. From the moment Child Protection Officer John Matthew Borovnik – the first person to uncover the mystery surrounding Tegan's whereabouts in 1999 – alerted Katoomba police to the fact he feared a child was missing, the case should have been made a priority. A crack team of highly skilled and experienced detectives was needed to get to the bottom of this unbelievable mystery.

A child cannot simply vanish into thin air – someone had to know something.

The problem was there was only one person who had all of the answers and that was the child's mother Keli Lane. Keli Lane who also just happened to be the daughter of a distinguished police officer,. Robert Lane. Keli's father was a well-liked member of the force and had spent much of his lengthy police career based on Sydney's Northern Beaches. Almost every officer on that beat knew him.

Manly Police Station was first alerted to the fact that Robert Lane's granddaughter was missing when they received the internal memo from their colleagues at Katoomba Police Station. The memo was signed by six of the Blue Mountains officers and sent on November 4, 1999 recommending that Keli Lane be interviewed. Contained in the memo was an explanation as to why the case had been referred to the Manly Station: it was the closest station to where Keli was living at the time with her parents and brother Morgan in Fairlight. It was a tricky case for Manly Police Station to handle, as Keli's father was well-known in the vicinity and had only recently retired from the force. It was one of those cases no one really wanted to land on their desk.

It ended up on the over-laden desk of Detective Senior Constable Mathew Kehoe. Already under pressure with his demanding workload, he took on the difficult and sensitive case of Tegan Lane too. But it wasn't until February 14, 2001 that he called Keli in for a formal, recorded interview – 15 months after he was handed the case. Detective Senior Constable Kehoe wasn't called to give evidence at the 2005 coronial inquest so it was never really explained why there had been such a lengthy delay in investigating the disappearance.

When Detective Senior Constable Kehoe rang Keli and asked her to come to the station for a chat, she did so voluntarily and without a lawyer. Before the interview began she was warned that her answers would be recorded and could be used in evidence against her – it was made extremely clear that she did not have to answer the questions if she chose not to.

Det. Sen. Con. Kehoe: "As I've explained to you, we're investigating a report forwarded to us in relation to the birth and subsequent adoption of that child [Tegan]."

Keli told the detective that the child was with its natural father Andrew Morris, whom she had met in December 1995 and had a brief affair with. She knew very little about him, she said, other than the fact that he had previously lived in Balmain. She remembered his birthday was some time in July or August 1966, because she recalled celebrating his 30th birthday the year Tegan was born.

Det. Sen. Con. Kehoe: "To your knowledge is there any reason why Andrew wanted to adopt or care for Tegan?"
Ms Lane: "He's the natural father and I was unable to take custody of her myself. And that was very clear from March in '96 when I found out I was pregnant, and I made that clear to him and that was part of the agreement between us, for me to carry the baby to full term."

Then Keli claimed that Andrew came to see her at Auburn Hospital on only two occasions. The first visit was the evening of Tegan's birth, when he came with his partner Mel and his mother. The visit was brief she explained, because they were hardly on speaking terms – actually they were practically strangers.

Even though the decision had been made that Andrew and his partner would care for Tegan, Keli stressed how much the couple now hated her. Mel could not stand the sight of her, she said, and Andrew "thought I was a big enough bitch and a hassle and a slut and all these things. Anyway he wanted absolutely nothing to do with me." It seemed puzzling to Detective Senior Constable Kehoe that a couple who felt such hatred toward Keli would then agree to take on the responsibility of her child. Surely it would be far too difficult for Mel to be reminded of her partner's unfaithfulness every time she looked at Tegan?

Det. Sen. Con. Kehoe: "Are you aware if his partner has any type of medical problem or she can't have children?"

Ms Lane: "No. It was just by choice because I was not able to have a child at the time, mentally or financially. I wasn't capable and wasn't prepared to keep Tegan, and Andrew was. He earned good money and he had a partner. They had a future together. Well, they indicated to me that they were going to be together, and I thought that would be more suitable than me on my own at university."

Again Keli claimed she saw Tegan on a number of occasions after the birth, but Andrew and Mel put a stop to her access about three or four months later. The last she had heard from them was in January or February of 1997. Keli explained that she no longer had an address for Andrew, however she thought she perhaps had a mobile phone number for him somewhere and promised to have a look for it. "That would be a start," said Kehoe. "When do you think you might be able to get back to us?"

"Well I can start looking tonight," Keli replied.

Detective Senior Constable Kehoe also pressed for the details on Tegan's birth certificate. Keli said she had signed the papers as Tegan L Lane, not Tegan L Morris. With the name of the father and a birth date, a hopeful Kehoe felt he had enough information to make a good start on the investigation. But like so many before him, and those to follow, he appeared to have been duped by the cunningness of Keli's deceptions.

As Keli left the police station that day, neither she nor Detective Senior Constable Kehoe had any idea that so much time would pass before anything was seriously done to track down the missing child. For soon after that formal chat with Keli, the busy detective was transferred to another station and the investigation into Tegan's whereabouts suspended.

Detective Senior Constable Richard Gaut was transferred to Manly Station in April 2002. He was immediately put to work on a missing person's case, but it was a suspected homicide – an adult female, feared to have met with foul play. Feeling he needed extra help, he made a call to the NSW Police Missing Persons Unit based in Parramatta, in Sydney's west, but he was informed that they already had a full workload and would not be able to assist. He was on his own.

It was while he was trying to solve the mystery surrounding the woman's disappearance, that Detective Senior Constable Gaut was handed the Tegan Lane file. It was October 9, 2002, five months after he had joined the team at Manly Police Station. Bearing in mind the Missing Persons Unit's less than enthusiastic reaction to his last request for assistance, he figured it would be easier to work alone and make his own inquiries. The first telephone call he made to Keli Lane was seven days later, but rather than call her in for a formal recorded interview, Detective Senior Constable Gaut decided to simply meet with her and check out a few details. "At that stage I had ordered a transcript of the provisional interview," he explained, "and I was simply getting Keli in at that stage to find out more information from her story."

Detective Senior Constable Gaut told Keli that police were having great trouble trying to locate Tegan, and that he'd also had no luck in tracking down the Andrew Morris she had named as the child's father. On hearing that Keli looked up shaking her head – his name was not Andrew Morris she said looking confused, it was actually Andrew Norris!

"I made a mistake," she said. "I told Detective Kehoe one name and I told you a different name." She said she had been confused

– the names sounded similar – but she was absolutely certain that the father's name was not Morris, it was Norris. This changed everything. The police had been looking for the wrong man. They were back to square one.

Then Keli threw another spanner in the works. She admitted that she had not been completely truthful with Detective Senior Constable Kehoe in the first interview. Tegan's "real" father Andrew Norris, as he was now known, had not dropped her home after she had handed over their baby in the hospital's car park; she had in fact caught a taxi. "I told him (Kehoe) what I wanted to have happened, that Andrew actually took me home. He didn't, he just left me there."

More than a year-and-a-half after she had promised to find a mobile phone number for Andrew, Detective Senior Constable Gaut asked her if she had managed to locate it. Her answer was no, she could not find it. However, there was another person she said who could verify her story: her close girlfriend Lisa Andreatta. Keli claimed Lisa knew Andrew from back in 1995 and 1996 and that she could back up Keli's story. As far as Keli could remember Lisa was the only person other than Andrew Norris, Tegan's father, who knew about the birth. Keli added that she hadn't seen her old university buddy for a long time though – the last she had heard Lisa was living in Queensland somewhere, but as she had promised the police with Andrew Norris, Keli made another promise to try and contact Lisa.

Promises, promises. So early in his investigation and dealings with Keli Lane, yet already Detective Senior Constable Gaut felt there were major discrepancies between the things that Keli had told Detective Senior Constable Kehoe and what he was hearing now. He realised it was imperative that he look into Keli's numerous stories more, before he called her in for a formal interview. "In that period I had to try and find witnesses which Keli had brought up, one being Lisa Andreatta… I realised at that point [that] Keli wasn't telling me the whole truth, so I had to make further inquiries and I suppose have as much information as possible before I interviewed her formally."

Detective Senior Constable Gaut's gut feeling was that Keli was lying and he was not sure if he could trust her. In the seven months between his informal chat with her and calling her in for a formal interview, he had tried to reach her by telephone on a number of occasions, leaving messages on her work and home answering service. They all went unanswered and he suspected that Keli was trying to avoid him. "I think I went on school camp," she would later explain. "I came back and there was a message on the school phone. I'd been away for a few days and then I went on school holidays."

But now Keli's life had taken a dramatic turn – one for the best for Keli, who it seemed, had at last found domestic bliss. By this stage Keli was engaged, and had a daughter with her fiancé. The three of them were happily living together. Keli's daughter, her fourth child who cannot be named for legal reasons, was the most precious thing in the world to her and it seemed that she had finally settled down.

There was one big problem though: her husband-to-be (whose identity is also protected) and their daughter, born in April 2001, knew nothing about her past.

It would be in a letter that Keli would eventually admit to receiving the calls from Detective Senior Constable Gaut, but even then she didn't pick up the phone and call him back. Instead she wrote to him to explain her delay in speaking to him.

December 13, 2002

Richard,

I have just returned from one long school camp. I received your message at home and will return your call on Monday. I also want to let you know that we are leaving for the UK on Saturday, the 21st of December, until January the 19th of 2003 to visit [my partner's] family for Christmas so they can see [our daughter], I am hoping in this time I can explain to them about Tegan when he is supported by his family members. I hope you understand the importance of this trip. I have details of our flights and a contact number while we are in the UK.

Thank you for your consideration.

KELI DID GO overseas, but even on the other side of the world she could not bring herself to reveal the dark secret she had hidden for so long from the man she loved. When they returned to Australia, her fiancé was still none the wiser, and it seemed that was the way Keli wanted to keep it. And she didn't make any attempt to contact Detective Senior Constable Gaut as she had promised to do either. Realising that Keli was avoiding him, the dogged detective eventually called her and asked her to come in for a formal interview. He informed Keli of her rights to obtain legal representation, but she declined the offer and came alone.

On May 9, 2003 Keli Lane arrived at Manly Police Station just before 10am and was taken to an interview room. Detective Senior Constable Gaut wanted to know why the people she was closest to were still in the dark about the investigation. The interview began at exactly 9:51am.

Det. Sen. Con. Gaut: "Is there any reason you haven't told him [your partner] about this matter?"
Ms Lane: "Because I don't want to break his heart."

THE IMPOSSIBLE task facing Detective Senior Constable Gaut was to determine which, if any, of Keli's stories were true. He pushed her to open up, demanding to know why she had not called him since returning from the European holiday. "Basically I just didn't want to upset everybody," she explained.

"Do you understand the importance of this matter – that we have to find out where your child is?" asked Detective Senior Constable Gaut. "Yes I do," she replied.

Keli admitted that she had lied to hospital staff about her family being in Perth and about having a boyfriend who was supportive and who had planned the pregnancy with her. Detective Senior Constable Gaut could not understand why she told such elaborate tales.

"I wasn't going to sit there and say no one was helping," she cried, distressed.

It was becoming very obvious that Keli had been feeling incredibly vulnerable and lonely in the final months of her pregnancy with Tegan. She said that all the lies she had told social worker Ms Baltra-Vasquez were simply a way to make a connection with the social worker. "I guess when I was talking to her, I wanted to try and talk with someone about how I felt at the time."

During the interview Keli became distressed at times, admitting she was surprised that no one had noticed her pregnancies or mentioned anything to her. "How do you tell people stuff like that?" she pleaded. "How can I say it's a second or third time? I'm not passing the blame, but how can people see me every day and not know? Not help? I couldn't, what, just walk up on the doorstep and go, 'Oh, hi, I had a baby yesterday.' Imagine what Duncan would do…"

Keli begged Detective Senior Constable Gaut not to tell her family, fearing they would have nothing to do with her if they knew the terrible truth. "You don't know what it's like," she cried. "I'm going to lose everything, I'll lose my job, [my partner]… I'll lose my parents … You don't know my dad, can you imagine what he will do? They wouldn't understand."

"I'm going to have to do a thorough investigation," Detective Senior Constable Gaut explained. "I'm going to have to start speaking with everybody – that includes your family and your friends. Now, I didn't want to have to go to that extent but I don't think you're being honest with me."

Growing up in a small community, cautious Keli knew exactly how the locals would react if they found out about the investigation and that's why she was so desperate to keep it quiet. A salacious story of love affairs, secret pregnancies and a missing child – she didn't think Manly was quite ready for so much scandal especially from the daughter of a respected local police officer. Once made public, Keli feared it would ruin not only her own reputation, but also that of her entire circle of family and friends.

"I'm asking you," continued Detective Senior Constable Gaut, "I don't know what's happened to the child and that's the problem. There are different versions you've told to different people along the way… It's very suspicious circumstances in which this child has gone missing. We've taken everything you've said at face value and we've made inquiries but we can't back up anything that you've said."

Keli was mumbling vaguely in reply to many of the detective's questions, so he decided that it was time to ask her directly what he seriously hoped was not true – that something sinister had happened to Tegan, that she was no longer alive.

"Did you kill the child?" he asked.

At that point in the interview Keli became clearly distressed, her voice jumped an octave and she was almost frantic in her reaction. "No, I did not. I did not do anything like that!"

But Detective Senior Constable Gaut was still not satisfied and bravely continued. "Did someone else [kill Tegan]?"

"No, no!" replied Keli.

The other likelihood that Detective Senior Constable Gaut was weighing up – among a variety of scenarios police were looking into – was whether Keli had sold her baby? Perhaps there was a grain of truth to the story of the Perth couple befriending Keli. Maybe a deal had been struck, freeing single mum Keli of the responsibility of rearing a baby on her own and avoiding the headache of going through the adoption process again and having to tell more lies. If Keli was feeling alone and desperate – as noted by her social worker – perhaps the offer of a sizeable amount of money in return for illegally handing over the child would have sounded like the perfect solution to her problems. Tegan goes to a good and loving home; Keli is financially sound and no one need ever know about what had taken place.

To test this theory, Keli was asked to provide her bank details to the police, which she readily did. Scouring her Westpac account, Detective Senior Constable Gaut could find no trace of any large inexplicable sums of money having been transferred.

Interestingly though, the account also showed that there had been no transactions at all within Keli's account around the time Tegan was born on September 12, 1996. Her account was not touched from May until October 2, 1996, which was 20 days after the birth.

It seemed odd that an account should have no activity for a five-month period (except for occasional withdrawal of bank fees).

Keli never did provide police with an explanation as to why she hadn't withdrawn or deposited money during that time frame.

It was this that Sergeant Rebbecca Becroft focused much of her attention on during the 2005 inquest. Sergeant Becroft was the counsel assisting the Coroner and basically ran the case – she questioned friends and family when they were on the stand and presented the police case to the court. With her deep, authoritative voice and directness, she ran an efficient court, but she was also friendly and sympathetic with witnesses – which was comforting for them, as most had never stepped foot in a courtroom before and found the process daunting.

At the same time Sergeant Becroft, just like Coroner John Abernethy, was determined to get to the bottom of the mystery and would press Keli and her family during questioning as far as she could go, to try and get some answers. Sergeant Becroft wanted to know how a person could survive for so long without touching their bank account.

"So it's fair to say that the account wasn't accessed?" Becroft asked Detective Senior Constable Gaut at the inquest. "That's correct" he replied. "That was the only banking record that you were provided with?" she continued. "That's right."

Detective Senior Constable Gaut was asked if he had checked with any other banks to see if Keli had another account, but no, he hadn't – to do so he would have to be issued with a search warrant for every bank, because there would be no way of knowing which financial institutions she had accounts with, and the chances of that many search warrants being issued was ludicrous, he claimed. "It would have been very difficult," he explained "to get search warrants on each bank if we didn't know that she had an account with that particular bank before applying for the search warrant, so they weren't done. We have taken on face value that that was the only account she's held."

Keli's friends and colleagues were asked about her spending habits around mid-to-late-1996, but no one could recall Keli having large wads of cash. Her friends suggested that would have been something they'd have noticed immediately, as they were all in their early twenties and didn't have much money. If Keli had suddenly started flashing a new wardrobe of clothes or a brand new car, or shouted drinks for them all they would have been suspicious.

As Detective Senior Constable Gaut's interview came to close, he told Keli that he was keeping an open mind about the information she had shared. Nevertheless he said he felt that: "The information you've given me makes me highly suspicious that something has happened to the child."

"Nothing has happened to her," replied Keli. "[Andrew] said he would contact me if there was an emergency, I have not heard cooee from them, not one word."

At the end of the 2003 police interview Keli was asked if she had anything further she wanted to share with the police. "I feel like I'm being backed into a corner and I feel uncomfortable," she explained. "I don't know what, I don't know what, oh I don't know what to say!"

The interview ended at 11:16am on May 9, 2003, after exactly one hour and 25 minutes of interrogation. Keli left on a promise that she would tell her parents and partner the truth about her past. Detective Senior Constable Gaut left the room knowing he had a great deal of work ahead of him.

It was to be some time before Detective Senior Constable Gaut tried to make contact with Keli again. In fact eight months passed during which he followed up a number of leads. But when he did try and telephone Keli his calls again went unanswered. That's when he made the decision to simply turn up on her doorstep at the house where she lived with her soon-to-be husband and their daughter. On Wednesday January 7, 2004 Detective Senior Constable Gaut knocked on her door accompanied by Detective Senior Constable Bradley Edgtton.

When Keli answered the door, the officers explained that they had been trying to reach her for a number of days and that it was important that she come to the police station either now or some time the next day for another chat.

With two police officers standing at her front door, Keli became noticeably anxious. Looking around to see if the neighbours were watching, she asked Gaut and Edgtton to please come inside. "Can you just come in so everyone doesn't hear what we're talking about?" she asked.

But Detective Senior Constable Gaut didn't want that to happen – he wanted every word spoken to be recorded at the police station. However he bowed to Keli's pleas because she appeared so agitated. The officers walked into the lounge room where Keli's daughter, her fourth child and the only one she has kept with her, was playing. Her fiancé was still at work. "I haven't heard from you in months," said Detective Senior Constable Gaut. "I was wondering why you haven't contacted me. I rang you yesterday and today and couldn't get through. I didn't want to have to come around here but I thought that you were avoiding my calls."

Keli was quick to explain herself. "My phone's been playing up, it's not just with you, it's with everyone. You can ring it if you want." But finding out the truth about the telephone was low on Detective Senior

Constable Gaut's list of priorities; he wanted answers from Keli. "Are you free to come down to Manly later today or tomorrow so we can go over where we're up to with our inquiries? There are a few things I want to ask you," he said.

It was agreed Keli couldn't accompany them immediately because she was unable to get a babysitter for her daughter, without having to explain the urgency, which she wasn't prepared to do. She figured her mother would be happy to mind her granddaughter though for a few hours in the morning, and a time of around 9am was organised.

"I can't understand why I haven't heard from you for so long," said Keli. "This is on my mind every day. I don't just sit around, I don't just sit at home when you don't call and not think about it."

Detective Senior Constable Gaut explained that there was a reason it was taking so long.

"I've had to follow up what you told me last time, we've had a murder inquiry and we have a lot of other cases all going on at the same time."

As the officers went to leave, Keli accused them of going behind her back and speaking to her friends about what had happened. "I've

The detective assured her no one intended to take away her child, but Keli became more upset. "There's no way, if my parents find out, that they'll let me keep her," she said.

got no friends now, nobody calls me anymore" she cried. "Keli I don't believe that is the case that you have no friends," said Detective Senior Constable Gaut patiently. "I suggested to everyone that I spoke to that this was a sensitive matter and asked them to put themselves in your position and treat the matter discreetly."

"One of them called me out of the blue the other day," Keli continued. "I hadn't seen her for three years. I don't understand why you have to speak to them, they don't know anything. They weren't even around at the time. What did they tell you? They didn't tell you anything did they?"

"Not a great deal," Detective Senior Constable Gaut admitted. "I'd like to speak with you about my inquiries but, like I said, I don't want to do an interview in your lounge room, I want to record everything, anything we say. I don't want to leave myself open to allegations that we made anything up."

Keli insisted that she would never do that, but Gaut made sure that she realised that there was a possibility that the matter would end up in court anyway. He was simply following proper police procedure.

At the thought of everything becoming public knowledge, Keli – visibly distressed – blurted out that she was getting married the following month and she was certain that if the matter ended up in court she would lose the daughter she and her husband-to-be adored. "If people find out that I gave a child away, sorry, there's no way they'll let me keep her."

But even after Detective Senior Constable Gaut tried to calm Keli by assuring her that no one intended to take away her child, she continued to get more and more upset. "There's no way, if my parents find out, that they'll let me keep her. They wouldn't understand about Andrew." Asking Keli if she wanted a glass of water to help settle her, Detective Senior Constable Gaut pointed out that there was little he could do to stop people finding out. "Keli it's out of my hands how other people react, but you told me in a letter a year ago you were going to tell [your partner]. If you're getting married next month and there's something you need to tell him about, it's better he hears it from you than from someone else."

As the magnitude of what lay ahead sank in, Keli's anxiety grew. "I'll be alone, I won't have anyone," she said. "I'll lose my job, there's no way a private school would keep someone on who gave away a child. What should I do, resign? Who do I talk to?"

Detective Senior Constable Gaut was in a very awkward situation – he was investigating a possible death, yet he was being asked to provide advice to a distressed Keli when he didn't believe that she was being truthful with him.

It was then that Detective Senior Constable Edgtton suggested that if Keli didn't feel comfortable talking to her family and friends, perhaps she should consider seeing a counsellor, and he suggested that the police could provide her with a number if she wanted to talk to someone anonymously. It wasn't the first time the police had offered Keli such help. The last time Detective Senior Constable Gaut had spoken to Keli he too had suggested she speak to a professional counsellor and had given her a phone number. She never called. It was obvious to the detectives that her demons had been manifesting in her mind with no outlet. Keli did say she had spoken to the school counsellor at Ravenswood, where she worked as a sports teacher, but she hadn't directly mentioned the secret pregnancies or anything to do with Tegan. In other words she hadn't whispered a word of the looming scandal to anyone. She was the lone guardian of her past.

Accepting she had to make another statement, Keli wanted to know what arrangements she should make for her daughter. "I feel I should prepare something," she said. "If this goes where you say it's going to go, and everybody knows, no one's going to let me stay with her. And I don't want a knock on my door and [they] just pull me away from her and [I] don't get to say goodbye to her properly or make sure she's okay."

But again, even after being assured that that was not going to happen – that her daughter wouldn't be taken from her – Keli couldn't relax. "In my heart of course I'm going to panic," she said.

Wanting to wrap up the informal talk as soon as possible, and believing it had already gone on much longer than he had wanted, Detective Senior Constable Gaut told Keli that she could come down to the station either that afternoon around 1pm, or the following morning at around 9:30am. It was agreed that the next day would be best.

True to her word, Keli was on time for what would be her third recorded interview with police. With the tape rolling at 9.38am, Detective Senior Constable Gaut wanted to clear something up from the previous day.

Det. Sen. Con. Gaut: "Why do you believe that they're going to take [your daughter] from you if this goes to the Coroner?"

Ms Lane: "It's just going to become a massive issue. Everybody's going to know, and my mum and dad and [my partner]. They're not going to want to be near me, are they? After everything they hear, I guess everything that you've looked into, that's just going to become public fodder. And who's going to let me stay with my daughter?"

Det. Sen. Con. Gaut: "No one's going to stop you from staying with your daughter."

Ms Lane: "I don't know if you're being kind or unrealistic."

Det. Sen. Con. Gaut: "Just what you touched on has given me the impression that [you think] if this goes to the Coroner's Court people are going to take your child away. I don't believe that's the case. If you've done something that you believe you are going to be in criminal trouble for, that [doesn't mean keeping] your child would be an issue."

Keli explained that her primary concern was her family's reaction to her sordid past becoming public knowledge – she believed it would be too much for them to bear. "Whatever the outcome is of anything, it is knowing what happened all those years ago will crush them," she explained. Keli was certain that once her parents knew what she had done they would throw her out and never speak to her again or let her see her daughter. "It's human nature, isn't it?" she added.

It was during the third interview that Detective Senior Constable Gaut was told a third version of how Keli got home from the hospital after giving birth to Tegan. Keli's previous two stories were firstly that Andrew, then known as Andrew Morris, had dropped her home in his car and then taken custody of Tegan. The second story was that he had just left her in the hospital car park and she had taken a taxi home. This time she claimed to have driven herself home to Gladesville – where she lived part of the time with her then boyfriend Duncan Gillies – in her car, although it was registered under Duncan's name. Keli said that she still had the car but no longer drove it as it wasn't registered and hadn't been for some time. It was parked on the side of the road in Mosman, one of the most affluent suburbs in Sydney's north (Keli never revealed why the car was parked in that suburb). "Are you prepared to allow us to forensically examine that car?" asked Detective Senior Constable Gaut. "You need to explain it a bit more, sorry," replied Keli, not completely understanding the officer's question.

It was at this stage that Keli realised she would need to seek the advice of a solicitor. She did not want police crawling all over the vehicle, until she understood what the consequences of that could be.

She couldn't ask her parents for advice because they were still in the dark about Tegan and the police investigation.

Detective Senior Constable Gaut, still optimistic that Tegan would be found, wanted to know if Keli would give police written permission to take a blood sample from Tegan. "Are you prepared to give a written consent for police to access the Guthrie card [the "Guthrie Spot" a standard procedure where a blood sample is taken from a newborn baby once it is 72 hours old, effectively making a note of the child's DNA] of Tegan Lane if we need to?" he asked.

"Maybe I should speak to someone about it, I'm not sure, I don't know enough about it," Keli replied nervously.

"What we're asking," explained Detective Senior Constable Gaut, "if we need to compare Tegan's DNA with anything as part of our inquiry to say either, for example, if we want to compare it with Duncan Gillies if he gives us DNA, to see if he was the father. That would probably be our main reason at this stage to want to do it, to be able to compare the two, and then that would tell us in black and white if Duncan's the father."

Panic was taking a grip of Keli. She had to get legal advice. She did not want the police poking around her car and now they were talking about blood samples. They were clearly deadly serious about this investigation.

It had suddenly dawned on Keli that she needed to check her rights and the implications of complying with the police requests.

Her dilemma raises the question: if Keli had sought legal advice in the first place, before agreeing to be interviewed by police, whether the case would have ever progressed to a coronial inquiry?

If she did have those thoughts in the back of her mind, it was way too late now.

"I find it unusual," Detective Senior Constable Gaut continued, "that you can be pregnant for nine months and living with a man and he doesn't know you're pregnant. That's why I've got real difficulty believing what you're telling me about Andrew Norris. I'm having real problems believing what you're telling me about Andrew Norris being the father and that Duncan Gillies knew nothing about it.

"When you were pregnant with Tegan were you showing?" Detective Senior Constable Gaut went on.

"I thought I was," Keli replied. "I'm a big girl anyway so it was very wide and a lot in my back, that's why I had all those rib pains apparently."

"Can you explain to me how Duncan did not know you were pregnant?" Detective Senior Constable Gaut pressed.

"I have no idea." Keli said adding that when she was pregnant with Tegan she saw a lot less of Duncan because both were busy with their sporting commitments.

Det. Sen. Con. Gaut: "Did you have any sort of sexual relationship around that time?"

Ms Lane: "I don't remember."

Det. Sen. Con. Gaut: "Were you sharing a bed?"

Ms Lane: "Yes."

Det. Sen. Con. Gaut: "Do you agree that, looking from an outsider's point of view, it would be very difficult [to imagine] how two people can share a bed and the girl's nine months pregnant and the man doesn't know? Do you agree with that?"

Ms Lane: "We never ever, ever discussed it. There was no indication to him or from him to me, whether it was a look or a touch, a word, nothing."

Detective Senior Constable Gaut just couldn't understand how K could conceal the pregnancy from her partner Duncan Gillies. "I just never was around him with my clothes off," she explained. "I'd get up early in the morning."

It was two hours and 14 minutes since Detective Senior Constable Gaut had begun recording his interview and feeling he had as much information as Keli was going to share with him that day, he decided to end the interview. "I've got real concerns with what you've told me," concluded Detective Senior Constable Gaut. "I find it hard to believe the story you've given me. If there's anything that you wish to tell me now before we stop this interview, if there's something you've been holding back from me, I urge you now to tell me."

"I don't have anything more to say," Keli replied.

It would be the last conversation Detective Senior Constable Gaut would have with Keli Lane.

so who is keli lane?
~~OLYMPIC DREAMS AND BABY NUMBER FOUR~~

chapter **4**

BORN ON March 21, 1975, Keli Lane seems to have had a perfectly idyllic childhood, one most people would envy. A blonde, athletic girl – something of a golden girl to her mum and dad – she grew up in a well-to-do suburb on Sydney's spectacular northern beaches. She was incredibly close to her parents Robert and Sandra, a conservative couple, and her little brother Morgan, three years her junior. Everyone in and around Manly knew the Lane family. Not only was her father – known to all as Bob – a respected local police officer, but he was also a champion sportsman in his earlier days.

Bob Lane was a bit of a local surfing legend and something of a whiz on the rugby field too. Indeed, it was a love of all sport that he would pass on in abundance to his two children. Drop in on any local sporting competition and you would undoubtedly find the Lane family there – sociable Bob and Sandra busy setting up the barbecue and chatting with other parents, while Keli and Morgan competed in the water and on the track.

From an early age Keli simply excelled at sport. She wasn't the sort of girl who clucked over her Barbie dolls or experimented with make-up with her girlfriends. If you wanted to find Keli, look to the great outdoors – there you would find her running around, whether it was kicking a ball or hanging out at the beach. She absolutely loved the water and was a natural at all water sports.

It was because of her love of everything athletic that Keli enjoyed school. Teachers liked having Keli Lane in their classroom because she was bright and always keen to learn. However her classmates were sometimes inclined to be envious, because she was good at nearly everything without seeming to need to make much effort.

One classmate remembered her as being a fiery, competitive tomboy, with a fine temper to boot. "It probably wasn't anything more than just being a kid," said the former classmate (who has asked that her identity be kept secret). "But sometimes she'd be nasty to the other girls. I don't mean she was violent in any way or anything, but she would put some of the other girls down and could get jealous."

Keli started at Mackellar Girls' High School in Manly Vale in 1987 where she quickly fell in with a group of friends who nicknamed themselves the "Six Pack". The group was inseparable and they helped each other through the mire of adolescence – talking about boys, crushes, sharing secrets... As they grew older there was nothing that they didn't know about each other, or at least that's what they thought.

When the scandal broke in local newspapers in October 2004 about the police investigation into ex-schoolmate Keli Lane, the rest of the "Six Pack" were gobsmacked. Immediately and individually each of them dismissed the story as a pack of lies – there was no way there could be any truth in it.

How could their friend have concealed pregnancies from her closest pals? How could all this have been going on right in front of their eyes without them knowing about it? It was impossible, and besides Keli would have confided in them – wouldn't she?

The telephone lines rang hot on the northern beaches the day the newspaper articles about Keli hit the stands. But although each of the girls must have spent hours with the handset glued to their ear, they didn't dare call Keli directly and ask her what they were dying to know – what had really happened?

When *The Daily Telegraph* contacted one of the girls on October 29, she said she wanted to remain anonymous. However she did admit that they were astonished that their friend had kept such a massive secret from them for more than a decade. Each of them was under the impression that they all knew everything about each other. How wrong they were.

One of the hardest things for the close-knit group of girls was hearing other people malign their friend in public, but being a small community it was inescapable. Keli Lane was the main topic of conversation at every local cafe, bar, hair salon and supermarket. It seemed everywhere they went Keli's "shameful behaviour" was being discussed by locals, who didn't know Keli as well as they did. And while even Keli's closest friends couldn't explain her actions – the facts of which they didn't doubt, even though it was incredibly hard to accept – they stood rock solid and supportive behind her. "She is from a good background with a loving family and loads of loyal friends,"

The telephone lines ran hot on the northern beaches the day the newspaper articles hit the stands. But none of Keli's friends dared to call and ask what they were dying to know.

one of the girls told *The Daily Telegraph*. "I just hope that people don't judge her as they don't know the Keli that we all know."

Certainly those closest to Keli protected her from allegations of promiscuity – they swear that that while she was growing up she didn't sleep around, (although there was plenty in Keli's life at the time that they didn't know about.) "Keli wasn't a tart or slut," the friend told *The Daily Telegraph*. "She had one or two steady, long-term boyfriends through high school and lots of good friends."

From her early teenage years Keli's size had been a bit of an issue. A natural athlete, big-boned Keli had a stocky frame, but was not overweight thanks to her endless sporting activities. It was because of her shape, size and sporting "uniform" that Keli was able to conceal her pregnancies, sticking to baggy tracksuits and never wearing tight fitting jeans or figure hugging T-shirts.

One of Keli's first boyfriends was Phillip Reber. The pair dated in 1994 when they were both 18 years old, but it only lasted four months and after the relationship ended they quickly lost contact. At the 2005 inquest into Tegan's disappearance, Mr Reber explained that he did not see Keli again for many years after they broke up and they never re-established any sexual contact.

The first Phillip knew of her pregnancies was when he read about them in the newspaper. Initially Mr Reber was of interest to police because of the timing of his relationship with Keli – he could have been the father of her first child, a girl, born in 1995.

"It's not something that you've thought to ask her?" Sergeant Becroft asked him at the inquest. "I haven't asked her, [but] of course it is, but I've got a family now. It's worried me and I haven't spoken to anyone really about it," he replied.

"Would you like to know whether you are the father of that child?" pursued Sergeant Becroft. "I don't know, I don't know," replied Phillip Reber.

No one regarded Keli's relationship with Phillip as being particularly serious, but that was not the case when she started seeing strapping rugby player Duncan Gillies in the latter part of 1994 when she was 19. From the very start, the relationship was intense and fast moving, and everyone who knew the couple believed they had each found their soul mate.

In fact when Keli's friends were to read about her pregnancies in the press, the first thought that entered their minds was that at least two of the children were Duncan's, because there was no way they could accept that Keli had cheated on him during their relationship between 1994 and 1998. They always seemed the perfect couple.

"She seemed really happy. I've never detected even a hint of sadness; she was such a happy-go-lucky person," said one of her friends during the same set of interviews in *The Daily Telegraph*. "I've seen her a lot over the years, at our school reunion, out and about at The Steyne Hotel or Manly. Never has she given any indication of what has happened in her life. She has always been happy to chat and be the wonderful person she is."

Keli and Duncan's relationship appeared so strong, that if anything, it seemed to pull Keli away from her girlfriends.

Kati Cummins was an old Mackellar Girls' High School friend of Keli's from 1987. Close in the early years, Kati clearly remembered Keli growing distant in 1996 and she put it down to her friend's relationship with Duncan Gillies. "She spent a lot of time with her boyfriend," Kati explained at the inquest.

But in common with some of Keli's other friends, she would have preferred to see their friend settle for a man who was more thoughtful towards Keli. "Duncan was a real boy's boy," Kati said, "and I didn't like him. He got on better with the boys than the girls. I don't know if that was a choice thing. He just played footy and he loved to laugh and he loved to just have a good time … and the way that we would socialise, it's always been the boys over in one corner doing their thing and the girls chatting in the other corner."

But whether Kati warmed to Duncan or not, it was obvious to her that Keli was deeply in love with him. From where Kati was standing, she saw that when Keli and Duncan were out together they had a lot of fun. "They were always the life of the party, I guess. They had a good time and they seemed to – yeah – they had a good time."

A sporting match, the couple clearly bonded through their passion for the outdoor life. Like Keli, Duncan was a dedicated athlete – a rising rugby and football star. He too had a heavy training timetable, and both played sport two afternoons a week, plus on weekends. When Duncan bought his first house in Gladesville in Sydney's inner west – a modest weatherboard property at number 10 Venus Street – Keli practically moved in, dividing her time between his house and the Lane family home in Fairlight. Duncan Gillies was already one of the Lane family: Keli's dad Bob Lane had been his rugby union coach when he was a lad and he would often stay at the Lanes' house on the weekend if he had a home game.

Growing up, Keli always held both her parents in high esteem, although her friends have spoken about Keli having a strained relationship at times with her mother. But Duncan Gillies maintained at the inquest that despite Keli being a serious athlete, there was never any parental pressure on her to win; only to do the best she could. "I don't think that Keli ever indicated to me that there was such a [pressure], but it's always there," he said. "She's a semi-professional sportsperson as I was and there is pressure to perform but I… in no way would I relate that to being sent down as a family message or family values that sport was the be all and end all."

Throughout Keli's four-year relationship with Duncan Gillies, she was financially dependent on her parents. It wasn't until she moved out of the family home in Fairlight in 2000, to live with the man who would father her fourth child and later become her husband, that she began to stand on her own two feet. When it came to money in the Lane household it was Sandra Lane who controlled the purse strings. If Keli needed cash, it was her mother that she would ask, although her father was a big softy and always good for a twenty or fifty dollar note if she was heading out with her friends. He rarely – if ever – said no to his daughter, he told the inquest.

On the surface Keli's life was an outward success. She had a close, loving and supportive family. She was earning herself a reputation as a talented and aggressive water-polo player, and seemed on track to realise her dream and represent Australia at the Sydney 2000 Olympic Games. Boyfriend Duncan Gillies was like-minded, with high hopes for a sporting future, wanting to play rugby professionally. As a couple, they made an impressive pair, both professionally and socially. Both were driven and determined in their respective sports, but equally a gregarious fun-loving pair always up for a good party or a drinking session on the weekends.

What dumbfounded quite so many professionals, friends and colleagues was how on earth Keli managed to hide her pregnancies from her nearest and dearest – baggy tracksuit pants or not. Indeed she was competing and training in just a swimsuit in the later stages of her pregnancies. With such a strong commitment to her sport, Keli continued to train up until the last possible moment. But as she began to struggle to hide her growing stomach, it did lead to a couple of comments and suspicions. A former water-polo coach remembered Keli skipping training for a couple of months around 1995 or 1996 and how completely out of character that was. Doctor's orders couldn't keep Keli away from the water he said, and as a competitor they didn't come any tougher than Keli Lane. "There were eyebrows raised,' he told *The Daily Telegraph* in October 2004. "People noticed she had put on weight, but then she went missing from training for a couple of months."

By this time Keli had left school and while she was still committed to her sport, she quickly realised she needed to find a way to pay the bills. She would need a career. Her eventual choice made plenty of sense – she wanted to be a PE teacher and at the beginning of 1996 enrolled in a Bachelor of Education, physical education course at the prestigious The Australian College of Physical Education at Homebush.

Lisa Gaye Andreatta started at the college the same year and the pair soon developed a close friendship. Together they tackled gymnastics and dance classes, and would often socialise out of class. Lisa met

Duncan Gillies on a number of occasions, but normally only when they were all out in a big group in Manly. "I really didn't think very highly of Duncan myself," she said at the inquest. "But they were in a relationship and they seemed to love each other, so that's their personal choice." Lisa preferred it when she and Keli drank at pubs in Balmain, because Duncan rarely came along. He did join them on a couple of occasions though at the Town Hall Hotel in Balmain, which was the pub sponsoring Keli's water-polo team – the Balmain Tigers – at that time. In all the nights they spent out together enjoying a few drinks, Lisa said she never saw Keli leave for a one-night stand or be overly flirtatious with any other men.

Keli and Lisa suspended their partying around September of their first year of university, to focus on their upcoming exams. It was because they weren't socialising together that Lisa didn't immediately realise that Keli had stopped coming to class. It was only from talking to a couple of the other students that she found out that Keli had withdrawn from the course.

"Did you speak to Keli about that withdrawal?" Lisa was asked by Sergeant Becroft. "No, [not] at the time," replied Lisa. "I tried to remember, like in September, it's our end of term anyway, so I didn't know really that she'd withdrawn and I knew that Duncan had a bad back around that time, so I just figured she was looking after him."

But Keli didn't return to the college the following term either. Another friend from the college said they had no idea she was pregnant and gave birth to a baby on September 12, 1996. "No one here knew she was pregnant. She kept it very well hidden. Everyone is completely shocked by this."

Incredibly, in the month before Tegan was born, Keli secured part-time work at Ravenswood School for Girls at Gordon in Sydney's north. She started on August 29, which was just two weeks before Tegan's birth.

An affluent and established school, the esteemed Ravenswood was built in January 1901 and originally focused on the strong academic education of girls with a solid religious foundation. In 1925 the school was purchased by the Methodist Church, reinforcing its Christian philosophy. It took in its first boarders 10 years later and has been a Uniting Church School since 1977.

For 30 years Ravenswood has been a Christian school catering for boarders and day students from kindergarten to year 12. According to the school's own website *"Ravenswood, as one of Australia's leading girls' schools, has a strong academic focus with an excellent and consistent record of academic achievement in the Higher School Certificate. Ours is a strong and supportive community with the capacity to get to know and care for the individual student."*

No place of authority or distinction enjoys being embroiled in a scandal and Ravenswood was certainly such a place.

Keli was initially employed to help coach the school's water-polo team. The sports' convener, Bronwyn Kim Friend, met Keli at the start of term four and they quickly became mates. Keli regarded the older teacher as a mentor and it wasn't long before she opened up to her and confided that she was having some personal problems with her relationship. When Keli and Duncan eventually broke up in March

Keli didn't talk to her colleagues about her pregnancy and, thinking it was her first, they put it down to nerves. They had no idea that this was to be her fourth baby.

1998, it was Mrs Friend who Keli turned to – she told her she was hurt about the split and that she was having some difficulties retrieving her belongings from Duncan's house.

Yet in all of their heartfelt conversations not once did Keli mention the fact that she was pregnant, and Mrs Friend certainly didn't suspect anything. But then again she had only ever seen Keli dressed in loose-fitting tracksuits and T-shirts. Mrs Friend left Ravenswood for a period in July 1999 – around the time Keli's third baby, a son, was born on May 31 that same year – however she was back at the school in 2001 when Keli started to show with her fourth child. Mrs Friend remembered it clearly because even though it was evident that Keli was several months pregnant, the young member of staff didn't discuss it with her or any of the other teachers. Believing it was her first pregnancy, her colleagues simply put Keli's refusal to talk about her pregnancy down to nerves. But they had no idea that this was to be her fourth baby. On the occasions a teacher did attempt to draw Keli into conversation about giving birth, she would become evasive, refusing to confide in anyone.

Nevertheless Keli was well-liked at Ravenswood. She was a popular and dedicated water-polo coach and developed a close rapport with the students. After three years working part-time, she was offered a full-time position and at the start of term one in 1999 accepted the role of teaching physical education, personal development and sport to the students. Ironically Keli Lane was proving to be a promising teacher – she was a mentor to the students in her care who clearly found her to be an inspirational icon in their school community.

Indeed Ravenswood students rave about Ms Lane in the school yearbooks of that year. Being younger than most of the other teachers at the school, Keli found it easy to relate to the girls. Even as she focused on her new full-time role, she continued to champion the school's water-polo program and the improved results under her watchful eye were a clear indication of her talents.

In the 2003 edition of the school yearbook Keli's beaming smile can be seen on one of the pages surrounded by her students. Former water-polo captain Rebecca Dinnie wrote: "A big thank you to Ms Lane for your encouragement and guidance throughout the season. Your support for every team has meant the strength in water-polo has grown immensely since last season."

And so the students at Ravenswood were naturally hugely distressed when news of the scandal and the police investigation into their sports mistress Keli Lane broke in the media. The girls were advised by their principal and teachers not to talk to journalists about the controversy. However a school spokesperson did confirm that the students were very upset about the matter. When approached by *The Daily Telegraph* in October 2004 the teacher refused to have her name published – simply saying: "I don't think it's fair to involve them [the children]. They're too young."

Under enormous public scrutiny a sad Keli felt forced to offer her resignation – effective immediately. Even after eight loyal years of service, there was no way she could stay on. The school had been unwittingly dragged into her mess and it would not tolerate having its name and reputation sullied. The school spokesperson Carole Boyden curtly told *The Sun-Herald* newspaper on March 5, 2006 "Keli went on voluntary leave from October 2004 and then resigned at the end of December that year. There are no plans for her to return."

But one of the parents of a girl in Keli's charge spoke more openly to me at the time the inquest got underway and admitted her daughter was quite distraught at the news. "It's been very difficult for her, for all her friends, they all loved Ms Lane and for this to happen is very distressing," she confided. "She doesn't quite understand how it could happen, and why Ms Lane didn't tell anyone, but I guess that's how we're all feeling, and we just hope it's cleared up. I don't suppose though that she'll be able to come back to the school, it would be too hard, and not fair on the students if she did, besides there's no way the school would employ her again."

Keli's old PE college friend Lisa Andreatta learned of the pregnancies before it was splashed across the front pages of Australian newspapers. She had received an email from Detective Senior Constable Gaut in March 2003 while travelling through North Africa and Europe. Lisa had left Australia in July 2002 and didn't return until July 2003. But incredibly, yet again, Keli had avoided an opportunity to tell her old PE pal face-to-face just three months before the email arrived – for Lisa had spent Christmas of 2002 with her old friend Keli in England and still Keli had not uttered a word about her dilemma. The pair spent four days together catching up and celebrating, but at no point did Keli confess to her old mate Lisa that she was being interviewed by the New South Wales Police back in Australia over the disappearance of a newborn. Still she kept her secret.

With Keli on her European trip was her fiancé, a man she had known for most of her life. At the 2005 inquest the Coroner put a suppression order in place, forbidding the media from publishing his name so as to protect the identity of the couple's young daughter.

Keli and her fiancé were childhood friends. Their parents had been friends since 1978. "We've sort of known each other since childhood," he told the inquest. He had been living in the UK, but when he moved back to Australia at the beginning of 2000, he moved in briefly with the Lane family. A few months later he and Keli decided to become flatmates and get a unit together, although at that stage they were not seeing each other romantically – it was strictly a platonic friendship. It wasn't until mid-way through that year that they started dating and jointly agreed that Keli would go on the contraceptive pill. But that didn't stop Keli from falling pregnant almost straight away.

When she broke the news to her partner in November – the first time she had ever been able to share news of a pregnancy and baby joy openly with anyone – she was already 16 weeks pregnant. Her husband remembers being surprised since he was certain she was on the pill. "I'm sure that Keli actually contracted measles roughly around that point" (suggesting a bout of measles may override the effect of a contraceptive pill), he explained to the inquest. "But whether or not that's the reason why she fell pregnant, you know I'm not a doctor." (When later, I asked Dr Rod Baber, an obstetrician at Royal North Shore Hospital about the possibility that measles may have been a factor in neutralising the effect of the contraceptive pill, he told me: "Unless there was significant vomiting or significant diarrhoea there would be no effect. Measles is just a mild viral illness. I can't imagine why it would have an effect.")

When questioned about the change in Keli's shape as her pregnancy progressed, her fiancé threw some light on how she had been able to conceal her previous pregnancies. The pregnancy had not been planned, but he still hadn't noticed any changes in her body shape before she told him about the baby. In the later stages of her pregnancy he did though see her shape change, but not in the same way as other pregnant women. "Oh you could see that she was pregnant at that point, it was more sort of width than, plainly obvious at the front there sort of thing."

Their daughter was born in April 2001. For Keli's fiancé it was the cherished moment most partners experience at the birth of their first baby and 20 months later the happy new dad proposed.

Had Keli been able to experience the joy of childbirth for the first time? Had she thought about her other three babies as she lay giving birth to baby number four, loving husband-to-be at her side? If she did, her fiancé was certainly none the wiser. Right now he felt as though he had the whole world at his feet – a baby daughter and the girl of his dreams had said yes to marriage. But he too was about to become dragged into Keli's unique nightmare.

In January 2004 with the wedding less than a month away, Keli still hadn't told her fiancé about the police investigation. By now it had been running for more than four years. Detective Senior Constable Gaut had been pressuring Keli to tell her fiancé for over a year and in the end threatened to do it himself if she didn't, as he was anxious to ask him a few questions.

When the dreaded conversation eventually took place Keli initially only confessed to the birth and subsequent disappearance of one child, Tegan, baby number two. But she was met with a stunned and emotional reaction to even a third of the truth. "Obviously my initial reaction was a state of shock, I guess," her husband later told the Coroner. "I certainly was unhappy at that time, but I wouldn't use the word betrayed – it's a bit harsh."

Although shocked and hurt, strangely Keli's fiancé didn't scream or shout, or even ask his future wife any deeply probing questions. He accepted what little she told him. "Obviously it was a big thing to take in at the time," he said. "She did obviously explain that there was an investigation in regards to the child and that if I had any questions I could speak to Detective Senior Constable Gaut about it. And on the day I called him he came around to our house."

Now Keli had to tell her husband the whole truth: she had given birth to two more babies, as well as Tegan. Unable to take quite so much on board all at once, Keli's fiancé decided he needed to take some time to seriously think about whether he wanted their marriage to go ahead. They had a gorgeous daughter together, but it was almost impossible to understand how and why his fiancé had kept such life-changing and dark secrets from him.

"Certainly I sort of questioned maybe what – what had happened at the time and maybe the reasons for those things, but you know initially it was a shock and – you know since then, our relationship has certainly got a lot stronger because of that," he said.

In the end he decided to go ahead with the planned wedding and while all those present described it as a joyous occasion, it's hard to believe the looming scandal didn't overshadow the day.

At that time the mystery was still very much under wraps, but the groom must have known that the net was closing in on his bride. It would be a further seven months before the "Keli Lane missing baby case" was made public, but no one could have predicted the media glare it would attract.

Now with her husband at her side, Keli was receiving some support and advice, and was no longer bearing the stress of the police investigation on her own. Her husband suggested that they see a solicitor and inquire about hiring a private investigator to try and track down Andrew Norris, the man Keli claimed was the father of Tegan – born, she said, after they had a brief affair. The couple approached Keli's solicitor Mary Bova who explained to them that such an exercise would be "prohibitively expensive." The newly-weds just didn't have that kind of money and so they were forced to drop the idea.

The strain of publicly standing by his wife was evident on Keli's husband's face throughout the inquest. He described his marriage to Keli as loving and honest and insisted that it was his personal decision not to question her about the pregnancies. He adamantly denied suggestions that she had put up a wall and refused to discuss what had happened. "Me trying to pressure her into trying to remember things isn't going to – well isn't going to assist her in remembering things," he reasoned. "So I haven't pushed the matter and obviously with the legal team they've tried to get as much information as possible."

"Have you asked her why she went through three pregnancies and legally adopted out baby number one and baby number three, why she didn't undertake that process for Tegan?" asked Sergeant Becroft. "Again we haven't discussed those kinds of details," he explained. "I'm comfortable with our relationship so it's not something that I think I will benefit from and I certainly don't think it will benefit us as a couple for me to delve into those details."

His insistence that he had no desire to know the details of his wife's secret past caused disbelief among the journalists who attended the court case each day. To us it was incomprehensible that Keli's husband had at no stage sat her down and demanded to know what had happened to Tegan, or why she hadn't terminated the pregnancies if she didn't want to keep the children. "It is a question that I do have," he said. "But again you know, the decisions I guess Keli took at those points in time, she thought were the best at the time. So again it's all sort of hindsight as to maybe what might have been the best decision to have made."

It was only after looking long and hard at the idea of continuing with their relationship, that Keli's husband decided to stay with her, he told the inquest. He became emotional as he explained that by the time he found out the true details of Keli's past, they had already forged a life: they had been together for three years and had a little girl – it was just too much to throw away. "From our relationship together, she's a fantastic wife, a wonderful mother and I love her dearly and there's no way in the world she would ever do something to harm a child."

In spite of knowing that her previous three children were the result of affairs, Keli's fiancé said he had never thought to question the paternity of his own daughter and that there was no way he would ask Keli to submit the child to a DNA test.

For many of Keli's friends and family, the media glare that inevitably accompanied the case was confronting and at times overwhelming. Kati Cummins broke down at the inquest:

"When it comes to this case, I don't want to form an opinion," she said tearfully as Keli started crying too. "I think as a friend all I can do is believe that what she is saying is the truth, and I do believe her. If I needed anything she would help me and would be there for me, and I hope that she knows that I'd be there for her. I don't want this to influence our friendship, of course it does, and it influences everyone around us at this time. It's taken over from a lot of things, we just – Keli said she didn't want to discuss it and, to be honest, I didn't particularly want to discuss it either."

Kati described her friend as the sort of girl who likes to keep herself to herself. "She's just private and she doesn't feel the need to discuss every little detail of her life and I respect – I respect her privacy. She knows she can tell me, and I just respect that she's a private person. Some people like to gab, I gab about everything. She's private, we're different in that respect."

Keli it seems hasn't "gabbed" to anyone.

the grilling of duncan gillies

AN INTIMATE AFFAIR

IT WAS KELI'S long-term boyfriend from 1994 to 1998, rugby player Duncan Donald Gillies who Detective Senior Constable Gaut always suspected was the real father of "missing" Tegan Lane, born in 1996. What's more he suspected Duncan may well be the father of her other two babies, born in 1995 and 1999, whom she had adopted out.

Besides the fact Keli had listed Duncan Gillies as the father of all three babies on their hospital records at the time of their birth, it was impossible for Detective Senior Constable Gaut to believe that Duncan could be sleeping in the same bed with a woman and not be aware she was pregnant. And even if he wasn't actually the biological father of the babies, Detective Senior Constable Gaut couldn't help but feel the rugby player was somehow involved in the disappearance of baby Tegan. When he wrote up his initial police report on October 2, 2003, Detective Senior Constable Gaut made several observations about the popular sportsman: he believed Mr Gillies was aware of the birth of Tegan, so much so, he put his suspicions in writing and signed the document.

He went into more detail about his suspicions at the 2005 inquest. "At that time I hadn't had the opportunity to speak to him [Duncan Gillies] in person, so there were a lot of questions which I hadn't been able to ask him."

Detective Senior Constable Gaut based much of his theory on evidence given to him by Mr Gillies' former housemate, Juan Carlos Ramirez. Mr Ramirez moved in to Duncan's Gladesville home in April 1996. Ironically it was at the insistence of Keli, who had recently met the water-polo player (Juan Ramirez) at a water-polo function. Mr Ramirez told police that he'd had a conversation with Duncan during which Duncan had told him that Keli was pregnant and had to go away, or was going away.

"I said to Duncan: 'What's up?' And Duncan said 'Keli's gone.' Duncan then told me that Keli either was pregnant or had been pregnant and that she had to go away. I can't recall which. He also said that they had to keep the pregnancy a secret from Keli's parents, as they would have been very disappointed. He told me that she had to go away because of the pregnancy. I can't recall exactly what Duncan told me, but I got the impression from the conversation that Keli was going somewhere to have the child and she was intending to give it away. It never came up in conversation as to whose child it was, but I got the impression it was his."

But Duncan Gillies denied that conversation ever took place. He claimed Mr Ramirez had only lived with him for a brief period and that he did not consider him to be a close friend. Mr Gillies said if he was going to confide in someone about something as big as Keli accidentally falling pregnant, it wouldn't have been Mr Ramirez.

Juan Ramirez went on to describe Duncan as "a bit of a player" to the police and said he suspected that his housemate was not faithful to Keli, although he had no concrete proof. "Well he was just a young guy full of testosterone or something [and he did] whatever men generally do, just go out. He gave me the impression that he – you know – had a few people that he would visit." He said by that he meant sleeping with other women.

But in a strange turn of events, when Mr Gillies heard from police what Mr Ramirez had said, he became suspicious himself – perhaps it was in fact Mr Ramirez who had fathered Tegan? He raised that possibility with the police, but a police check with immigration knocked that possibility out of the ring straight away – Mr Ramirez was overseas when Tegan was conceived (around November or December in 1995); he only came to Australia to play water-polo in January 1996. Sergeant Becroft asked Duncan Gillies if he had suspected Mr Ramirez could be the father at the inquest. He said yes, but she informed him why it was not possible.

Detective Senior Constable Gaut was basing much of his early investigation on this alleged conversation between Duncan Gillies and his former housemate Juan Ramirez. When Detective Senior Constable Gaut told Keli about the chat he had with Mr Ramirez, she was genuinely shocked. She was certain that Duncan was absolutely clueless about the pregnancies, so could not have talked about her being pregnant to Mr Ramirez. "Why didn't he help me then?" she asked. "If he knew, why didn't he help me?"

It certainly appeared that whether he did or didn't know about the pregnancies, Duncan Gillies was the rock Keli Lane wanted to lean on – whether she could or could not – in times of trouble. During her police interview in 2004 Keli was asked why she had listed Duncan as the father on all three hospital records, yet not once during the nine months of any of her pregnancies did she ever mention to him that she was having a child? Keli explained that she didn't want anyone to call Duncan – accepted, the telephone number she always gave for him was incorrect – however, if something had gone wrong with the birth, she wanted him to be alerted. She figured by only giving his name, and not a correct contact number, finding him would involve a great deal of effort – and hospital staff would only do that if desperate. "I wanted him to be there if something was going to happen to me, if I was going to die or something... I almost did."

Detective Senior Constable Gaut was surprised to hear Keli talk about any possibility of her dying during childbirth and wanted to know what she meant – according to her records while there were complications with the birth of Tegan, there was no mention of her being seriously ill. "They said I was very sick," she explained. "I had a haemorrhage and the doctor had to come in and they said 'You were pretty sick', like there was a lot of blood."

Keli also insisted that the statement from water-polo player Juan Ramirez to Detective Senior Constable Gaut that his then-housemate Duncan Gillies knew Keli was pregnant, was a total fabrication. "I don't believe it," she said adamantly. "Duncan wouldn't let me struggle like that by myself. No, I don't believe that. I don't believe that Duncan wouldn't even say to me, 'Do you need help, or do you need a hand?'" Detective Senior Constable Gaut asked why Juan Ramirez would lie to him. "I'm totally shocked," said Keli at a loss. "I'm totally shocked, I don't understand. If Duncan knew why didn't he say something to me or support me, if he knew what the issue was then why wouldn't he have helped me?"

When Juan Ramirez was called to give evidence at the 2005 inquest, to publicly back the comments he had made to police about Duncan knowing Keli was pregnant, he appeared nervous and forgetful. Immediately he began to backtrack on his previous statement to the police, saying he was no longer certain that it had taken place.

"You know," he said, "I was thinking at that time. I can't be certain ... it's only something that has just been playing in the back of my mind, that I had a conversation with Duncan."

But the police statement Mr Ramirez signed on November 14, 2003 – as a true and accurate account of what he believed had transpired between him and Duncan – was very direct and specific about what was discussed in Duncan's lounge room.

Sgt. Becroft: "You just seem a little evasive. Are you scared that you're going to get into trouble for telling us exactly what the conversation was about?"

Mr Ramirez: "No, that's not why I'm scared, I guess I'm just worried if that is exactly what I remember hearing... It's like, am I really certain about it? Because in those days – and in my life at that time I was just kind of living just to get by and – you know – whatever people were doing around me, I didn't really care. I was more or less casual about what I was doing. If he was having problems, bills or he had problems otherwise, or if Keli had problems, I didn't really care because there was no real connection for myself with her or with Duncan."

Only Duncan Gillies could reveal the truth about his relationship with Keli Lane. Keli, the former girlfriend who still relied on him so much, that she insisted on his name being on her hospital records during all three pregnancies. That way he would be the first to know should her life be in danger during childbirth.

It was vital that Mr Gillies clear up the great deal of confusion in Detective Senior Constable Gaut's mind. When he had last formally interviewed Keli on Thursday January 8, 2004, her third formal interview, Detective Senior Constable Gaut was relying on information about Mr Gillies relayed back from Ireland, where Duncan Gillies had been living with his wife since 1998.

He was interviewed by Detective Richard White of the Garda, Ireland's national police service, in the year 2000, at Cobh Garda

Station in County Cork. Detective Senior Constable Gaut did not directly interview Mr Gillies until December 2004.

For some reason word had come back from the Garda that Duncan Gillies had admitted to being the father of the first child, the baby girl born on March 19, 1995. In fact Mr Gillies had simply said he was aware of Keli's third pregnancy, after being informed by Virginia Fung in 1999 via a letter sent to Manly Rugby Football Club. It was based on the erroneous statement from the Garda– and still believing water-polo player Juan Ramirez's statement that Duncan Gillies knew of baby number two Tegan – that Detective Senior Constable Gaut quizzed Keli abut her "true" relationship with Duncan Gillies.

During that final formal interview with Keli, Detective Senior Constable Gaut demanded: "You're going out with Duncan Gillies, you've had a baby, you've had no support. You've had to adopt the child out, yet I've got an interview with Duncan Gillies where he's saying that he's the father of the first child. So what I'm looking at [with Tegan] is a person who's taken no responsibility for the first child, and then you find yourself pregnant a year later and you go to hospital by yourself. You're telling different people different stories, which are total, total lies [the] lot of them."

But baffled Keli was insistent that Mr Gillies didn't know about any of the pregnancies and she couldn't provide an explanation for what he had reportedly told Irish police.

"I find it very hard," said Detective Senior Constable Gaut, "to believe that a girl can have a number of children and be living with a man and he doesn't know anything about this."

It seemed the answers would have to come directly from Duncan Gillies himself.

The day Duncan Gillies was listed to give evidence at the inquest, the courtroom was packed – everyone was jostling for a seat, eager to hear him explain how it had escaped his attention that his girlfriend was pregnant, and a couple of times too. Sceptical at the best of times, the journalists covering the case found it impossible to believe that a man could have a sexual relationship with the same woman for four years and not notice drastic changes in her body shape. Before seeing him give evidence surely not one person in that courtroom could have believed that he wasn't somehow involved.

On the morning Duncan Gillies showed up at court, the television crews crowded the front steps and while no one had any idea what he looked like, as soon as he stepped out of the car, there was no doubting that this was the man at the centre of the saga. After years of playing professional rugby, Duncan Gillies still had a powerfully built body, standing more than six feet tall with broad shoulders, dark hair and strong features.

He walked toward the court with an imposing manner – yet surely his outward confidence belied an inner fear? He was about to swear on *The Bible* and take an oath, then face his now notorious ex-girlfriend and reveal deeply personal details about their love life.

To cap it all, Duncan Gillies' new wife Karen was with him, she was at his side, and she too would hear all the intimate details of his sexual experiences with Keli – as would his old rugby and school mates. The next day he would wake up to a media frenzy, as the front pages of all the newspapers were splashed with the private sex secrets of Duncan Gillies and Keli Lane. It was hardly the homecoming he had hoped for, but it was an embarrassing scenario, which his wife appeared to handle much better than he did. With her freshly groomed hair, stylish suit and oversized glasses, the calm, collected petite blonde couldn't have looked more unlike her husband's stocky former lover. All they had in common it seemed was the colour of their hair and the fact they could have exchanged notes on Duncan Gillies' bedroom antics.

When he took the stand he explained how "in love" he had been with Keli and how perfect he believed the relationship was. "I know at the start of the relationship and in the first few months of the relationship we did talk about how much in love we were," he explained, "and that it was amazing that so quickly we could be thinking of marriage."

Keli and Mr Gillies started a sexual relationship as soon as they met, and while he couldn't remember the exact date, he did remember that it was the night after the first round of the rugby competition in 1994 when his team Manly played Drummoyne. "I think consistently, you see in the world I was living, in the relationship I was having with Keli the two of us were madly in love. Now there was obviously, we now know, there was something else going on, but take it as you will, I didn't know it was going on. So I'm stuck in this, I'm in this relationship where I'm madly in love. We enjoyed each other immensely. We always had a great time together, fought rarely and yes of course I'm sure if we had fallen pregnant outside of wedlock I would have jumped at the chance."

Duncan Gillies said he was not only rocked by the news that Keli had given birth to a baby in 1996 who had since disappeared, but that he had also known nothing at the time about the baby girl born previously in 1995. He was insistent that despite still enjoying a sexual relationship with Keli between 1994 and 1998, he hadn't ever noticed the pregnancies. "I had no comprehension whatsoever that she has had two babies while I was sleeping with her, for the four years we were going out."

Sergeant Becroft apologised to Mr Gillies for forcing him to reveal intimate details about their sex life but insisted it was imperative to the investigation.

Sgt. Becroft: "Did you ever see Keli naked without her clothes on?
Mr Gillies: "Yes I did see Keli naked with her clothes off but at no time did I assume she could have been pregnant."
Sgt. Becroft: "Did you form the view that she changed her physical body shape in the fact she may have put on weight?"
Mr Gillies: "I'm sure she did."

The atmosphere in the courtroom became visibly tense and uncomfortable when Mr Gillies was then asked to explain his sex life with Keli in detail. His wife shifted rigidly in her seat when he retorted "what, you want a demonstration?"

Obviously furious at being asked to share the intimacies of his relationship, he explained that he and Keli had often had sexual intercourse in the "spoon" position. "I mean we're lying down, sex is from behind, it's not the missionary position, it's not any other position, we're lying down. I'm cuddling into Keli's back."

Mr Gillies said that he remembered on a number of occasions when he went to put his hand around her front to embrace her by touching her stomach, that she would push his hand away and tell him not to, because she was putting on weight. It didn't raise any suspicions though – he simply put it down to being a "girl thing". He said that Keli's weight would often fluctuate during their relationship, but it was just something that as a man he was smart to avoid commenting on. "So, say when she got up in the morning, did she quickly get dressed so that you couldn't see her?" asked Sergeant Becroft. "I wasn't living with the predetermined spy attitude where I would catch her," he explained. "You have to imagine I never thought any of this was happening, so at no stage was I trying to put the pieces together. She could quite easily have jumped out of bed, whipped on the tracksuit and said 'I've got to go home, it's late.' She could have done that for the six months she wasn't pregnant, and it wouldn't have made a difference ... I wasn't looking for anything."

He shook his head in frustration as he accepted how incredible it all sounded. "I understand how it looks... It seems ridiculous coming out of my mouth as it just seems [like] commonsense that I would pick up on her having a baby."

When Sergeant Becroft pushed Duncan Gillies to remember anything odd about Keli's behaviour, he seemed to flare up and appeared ready to lose his temper. "I wasn't skulking around in the dark to see if the woman I loved was having babies out the back door," he retorted.

It was social worker Virginia Fung, from the Anglicare Adoption Services at Telopea, Parramatta, who had informed Duncan Gillies that Keli had given birth to a son in May 1999, when Ms Fung had innocently sent him a letter requesting formal permission to go ahead with the adoption of the baby boy. Keli had told Ms Fung that the father of her child was her boyfriend Duncan Gillies and the reason she could not keep the baby was because she wanted to move to London to live for a short time. Ms Fung, not convinced that Keli really wanted to give up the baby boy, back in 1999, had tried to hunt down Duncan Gillies who was listed as the child's father. Despite being given a wrong telephone number, she finally reached him by way of a letter sent to his rugby club.

Said Mr Gillies: "I received a letter via the Manly Rugby Club from the DoCS and from that letter I rang the the DoCS. Basically the letter said: 'You're the father of a child that's going to be adopted out. Is it okay if we adopt your child out?' I rang the DoCS and said 'Look to the best of my knowledge I'm not the father of any child.' And [the woman] said: 'You are listed here as the father of this child.' And I said 'right, leave it with me for a couple of days and I'll get back to you.' And in the meantime my current wife and I spoke with Keli."

That conversation was – as one would expect – incredibly awkward, and it was agreed that Keli would remove Duncan Gillies' name as the father of the child the DoCS was trying to adopt out. He knew there was no way he could have fathered the child because his relationship

Duncan Gillies was asked how he could not have known that the woman he lived with was pregnant. "I understand how it looks," he said, "it seems ridiculous ..."

with Keli had ended in March of 1998, 14 months before the birth of the child.

Sgt. Becroft: "Had you had any sexual relationship with Keli after you'd broken up with her?"

Mr Gillies: "No."

Sgt. Becroft: "So therefore it would be impossible for you to be the father of [the child]?"

Mr Gillies: "That's correct, yes."

It may have been impossible for Mr Gillies to have fathered Keli's third child, the boy, but at this point in the minds of the police, it was still highly probable that Duncan Gillies was the father of her first born girl or second born girl, missing Tegan.

It wasn't until 2004 – when Keli's first born daughter, was nine years old – that Duncan Gillies was asked to participate in a paternity test. A DNA sample was obtained, but the result was surprising to all, except perhaps Keli. Mr Gillies was not a match – he was no relation to the little girl born on March 19, 1995.

Sgt. Becroft: "So it's the case that obviously then, some time during your relationship with Keli in 1994 and 1995, that another man has fathered Keli's child?"

Mr Gillies: "Yes."

Sgt. Becroft: "Are you aware of who that man is?"

Mr Gillies: "I am not."

Sgt. Becroft: "Were you aware of Keli having an extramarital affair?"

Mr Gillies: "Most certainly not."

Sgt. Becroft: "Did you suspect she was having an affair?"

Mr Gillies: "Never."

For Duncan Gillies hearing that his girlfriend of four years cheated on him at least twice during their relationship was gut wrenching.

He was asked about his movements around the time that Tegan was conceived in late 1995.

"I have a fairly good idea of what I was doing the whole time," he said. "I was actually out there just living life and having a great time and taking every opportunity that came towards me."

From his recollection – and his bank statements backed his claim – he was on a three-week shooting trip with some buddies in country New South Wales in December. He said he spent quite a bit of time in Armidale and believed that at Christmas he was working at The New England Hotel (in Armidale) with one of his mates.

He went on to tell the inquest that he had no idea who had fathered any of Keli's children, as it had never entered his mind that she was being unfaithful to him and he wasn't on the look out for any suspicious activity.

Mr Gillies also denied police claims that he was the person who wheeled Keli into the emergency ward of the Royal Prince Alfred Hospital, when she was about to give birth to her first child – even though staff records make a reference to her boyfriend doing just that. That was something Keli also strenuously denied, claiming she couldn't remember who it was, but she was 100 per cent certain it wasn't Duncan. She said it was more likely to have been a taxi driver.

In trying to determine what, if any, role Duncan Gillies had played in the disappearance of Tegan, Detective Senior Constable Gaut spoke to many of his family members. He was intrigued by a conversation Mr Gillies' brother Simon and his partner Narelle said they had with Duncan and Keli. Simon recalled that some time in 1995 or 1996, the four of them had talked about whether it was a good idea for Duncan and Keli to have a child. Detective Senior Constable Gaut believed that went some way to backing his suspicions that Duncan Gillies was possibly Tegan's father.

Still Mr Gillies was forceful in his belief that if any of the children had been his, Keli would have felt comfortable enough to tell him and they would have worked it out together. He explained to the Coroner that he felt if Keli had fallen pregnant and told him, they would have got married and kept the child. He was adamant that he would not have put any pressure on Keli to terminate the pregnancy.

"Have you spoken to Keli about abortion?" Sergeant Becroft asked him. "No," he replied.

Unable to face the fact that the young love of his life had lived a secret life which he had no knowledge of, and knowing she had been involved with at least one other man, Mr Gillies found it very difficult to make eye contact with Keli – who was sitting less than five metres from him in court and was in his direct line of sight. She rarely looked at him while he gave his evidence, or reacted to anything he said. She would simply hold her father's hand from time to time for reassurance.

"Since you became aware of all this, it must have been a hell of a shock?" Sergeant Becroft asked Mr Gillies. "A hell of a shock is a bit of an understatement," he scoffed. "Just to clear the matter up," he continued, "if I was aware in any way that Keli was having an affair I would have ceased [our] relationship."

For all his harsh judgments of Keli's actions during their relationship, Duncan Gillies wasn't exactly whiter than white either. He too had been unfaithful, and scandalously it was with one of Keli's close friends, Tarryn Woods who went on to win Gold at the Sydney Olympics Games 2000 in water-polo.

The one-night affair took place after a surf club carnival at Freshwater beach on Sydney's northern beaches. The pair went home together to the unit Mr Gillies was then sharing with a friend at Manly. Being part of a small circle of friends, and fearing news of his infidelity would eventually leak out, Mr Gillies confessed to Keli.

Sgt. Becroft: "How did Keli react when she found out that it was Tarryn Woods?"

Mr Gillies: "I don't think she was overly surprised. To be quite honest

Keli had warned me before that Tarryn had attached herself to other girlfriends' boyfriends and I swore that [it wouldn't] be a problem with me and that I'd be awake to that, but unfortunately on this specific night I wasn't."

Mr Gillies claimed that Keli took the news relatively calmly and while she was incredibly upset she did forgive him, saying: "You're not getting away from me that easily."

But Duncan Gillies' affair with Ms Woods happened quite early in his four-year relationship with Keli Lane, at a time when those around them had believed their relationship to be at its strongest. They were spending nearly all of their spare time together and Duncan Gillies was a frequent guest at the Lane home in Fairlight, happily kicking back and enjoying a family dinner on regular nights. In 1994 and well into 1995 Mr Gillies was playing rugby for Manly. With training every Thursday night and home games every second weekend – and at that time he had yet to buy his home in Venus Street, Gladesville – he also found it was convenient to spend those nights at Keli's family home in Fairlight.

"I'm going back to the club and having a few beers and staying at Keli's place," Mr Gillies said. "On Thursday nights I'm going back to the club, having a feed and a few beers and probably staying at Keli's place again. As opposed to in 1996 when I would be lucky to see her on weekends. She would have had to come to where I was, as opposed to me going to Manly to play a home game."

The reason the couple saw less of each of each in 1996 was because Duncan Gillies was picked up to play for the Canterbury-Bankstown Rugby League Club (The Bulldogs Rugby League team), which is why he made the decision to buy a property in Sydney's inner west. Things didn't go to plan though and he was dropped from the premiership competition into the metro cup competition, which meant travelling even further west for training three times a week and Saturday games. With his busy schedule and Keli's water-polo commitments it left little time for romance.

Sgt. Becroft: "What about during the week with her connection to Balmain water-polo and its proximity to Gladesville?"

Mr Gillies: "Yes she would drop in and she'd beep the horn outside. We would keep in contact ... but geographically there's a great distance (and) it just wasn't working as easy."

Sgt. Becroft: "So you don't believe you were, and I don't want to put words into your mouth, you don't believe there were that many sleepovers in 1996?"

Mr Gillies: "I don't know if there was or wasn't but looking back at the evidence of where I was and what I was doing I would have to say there was certainly far less than what there was probably the previous two years or even in 1997. I can see how when she was coming towards full term she probably wouldn't come into the house, she might beep the horn outside and I would see her out the window, run out and give her a kiss. She'd say, 'I've got to go to training, I've got to go here, I've got to go there.'"

Facing pregnancy was not something Duncan Gillies had seriously considered during his four-year relationship with Keli, because he knew she was on the contraceptive pill. He had seen the packets of pills in her bag a number of times and he frequently saw her take it. It was the only form of contraception that they used.

Since learning about the pregnancies, Mr Gillies said he had gone over and over in his mind to recall if there was anything odd about Keli at the time. He said there were a few occasions when he remembered she was quite erratic in her behaviour. At the time he hadn't thought much of it, but in hindsight he believed it was shortly after the birth of baby number two, Tegan, in September 1996.

"There was a comment by Keli's father at one stage in the house," he said, "where Bob Lane mentioned: 'You're looking beautiful, Keli, don't put all that weight on again' and Keli got more than flustered that it was a reference to weight. You have to understand this is all in hindsight. Of course she was going to be temperamental about her weight – it's a feminine gift, but for her to [react like that], looking back now I can see that it meant something else to her."

But the big mystery still confounding the police, concerned the crucial two hours between Keli Lane checking herself out of Auburn Hospital – at around 2pm on Saturday September 14, 1996 and arriving at the wedding of close friends Craig and Dianne Hansen in Manly at

4pm with Duncan Gillies. Struggling to remember back to that day, he thought from memory that he had driven his Ford F100 truck to the wedding, and parked it under a tree at a nearby school shortly before 4pm. But as much as he tried he just couldn't recall to the court whether he had picked Keli up or not. Nor could he recall if she had dressed at his home, or if she had just met him at the church.

That was different to the version given by Keli's mother, Sandra, who said that she had dropped them off together and that Keli had dressed at her parents' home where Duncan was waiting for her.

It was at this point that the coroner himself, John Abernethy, interjected with his own line of questioning.

Coroner Abernethy: "Do you remember, and again this is a big ask, do you remember what happened after the wedding, after the reception? Just keep in mind Keli's just had a baby and come out of hospital that day."

Mr Gillies: "I don't remember but my guess would have been me returning to the Lanes's house in Fairlight."

Mr Gillies made no reference to Keli's behaviour at the wedding, behaviour that may have hinted at her inner turmoil, to the fact that she had given birth only a few hours earlier. To his mind she appeared fine and he certainly didn't suspect that she was the mother of a newborn.

In fact, when Duncan Gillies was first told of Keli's 1999 pregnancy by social worker Virginia Fung he was incredulous. As far as he was concerned the Keli he knew had never been pregnant. In agreement with his wife he telephoned Keli to ask what was going on, and to have his name removed from the adoption papers.

He even went on to tell the Coroner that at that time (in 1999) he believed Keli had just been covering for a friend who was in trouble herself. He figured the most likely story was that she had helped someone escape going through the hospital system. Keli had, he thought, allowed this mythical person to use Keli's name and therefore protect her own identity.

"I couldn't believe it could be Keli," Mr Gillies told the inquest. In his mind this whole fiasco led to the adoption agency's letter to

Keli Lane in 2005 attending Sydney's Westmead Coroner's Court, where she was the focus of intense media speculation. The coronial inquest into the suspected death of her baby, Tegan Lane, came about because police had pretty much come to a dead end with their investigation. Keli had initially cooperated with detectives but stopped talking on the advice of her lawyer.

Keli Lane was interviewed by police on 9th May 2003. It was her second of three recorded interviews. In an ever deepening mystery, Detective Senior Constable Gaut was drawn into a web of evasion, half-truths and, as he soon suspected, outright lies.

In her interview with Detective Senior Constable Gaut Keli insisted that a man called Andrew Norris had fathered baby Tegan during a short-lived fling. To the police he sounded like an all-round scoundrel – but, much more significantly, no one could find him.

Keli Lane leaving Westmead Coroner's Court with her father, Robert Lane, in 2005. Each day as Keli struggled through the throng of newspaper reporters and cameramen, he held her hand firmly, walking beside her, always staring straight ahead.

At the inquest Robert Lane explained how he and his wife had been floored when Keli eventually told them about Tegan. "In hindsight I feel a bit foolish," he said, "in that I didn't notice a thing. But I'd had no reason to believe she was pregnant at all."

Detective Senior Constable Richard Gaut at a press conference on 27th June 2005, just minutes after the coroner adjourned the case to allow police more time to gather evidence. It was yet another delay in a case that had brought endless difficulties.

Sergeant Rebbecca Becroft meets the press. As counsel assisting the Coroner she played a key role in the inquest. On one notable occasion she had to apologise to witness Duncan Gillies for asking him about intimate details of his sex life with Keli Lane.

Keli's lawyer Peter Hamill arrives at Westmead Coroner's Court. He pounced on the mix-up over the last name of the alleged father of Tegan. Was it "Andrew Norris" or "Andrew Morris"? Mr Hamill insisted that the mistake had been made by police.

Left DoCS worker John Borovnik whose vigilance first aroused suspicions about the fate of baby Tegan. **Right** John Abernethy ended his long career as NSW State Coroner with this case. "We hit a dead end," he said later. "We just couldn't figure it out."

Keli Lane's family were witnesses at the inquest. Her brother, Morgan Lane, said he didn't want to ask Keli what had happened. Her mother, Sandra, though clearly uncomfortable throughout the proceedings, was able to give the court vital evidence on oath.

Left Duncan Gillies and his wife Karen arrive at the Coroner's Court on 24th June 2005 to give his much anticipated evidence. **Right** Julie Melville (Duncan's mother) leaves court. Despite being listed as Keli's midwife, she knew nothing about the pregnancies.

Kati Cummins leaves court after giving evidence on behalf of her friend Keli. She told the court that Keli was a "fabulous mother" and that she believed her story. "I think as a friend all I can do is believe that what she is saying is the truth, and I do believe her."

Olympic water polo player Tarryn Woods leaves the inquest on 13th February 2006. With team-mate Stacey Gaylard, suspecting from Keli's torso that she was pregnant, Tarryn donned goggles and dived into the pool to take a closer underwater look at her.

Auburn Hospital, in Sydney's west, where Keli gave birth to Tegan in 1996. Two days later she discharged herself. How did a popular, fun-loving girl from a well-to-do, close-knit family end up in this place: utterly alone, on "the other side of the tracks"?

Keli at the wedding of her friend's Craig and Dianne Hansen, just two hours after leaving hospital. Her friends and family had no idea about her new baby, or even about her pregnancy, and at that point it must have seemed to Keli that they never would.

his rugby club asking if he was in agreement that his so-called son be adopted.

It wasn't until four years later that he was forced to face the truth. "Yeah, that had been resolved," he said. "And that was the end of that little piece. But then the DoCS worked out that she'd had two earlier pregnancies. I was under the impression for such a long time that it was just virtually impossible, as I'm sure you're all thinking, for me to be in this relationship and not notice that she was pregnant. So my line of thought went to [the belief that] she was helping someone else [and that] she wasn't pregnant. I've had a four-year battle with that acceptance. Up until about May 2004 I thought it was just virtually impossible that she would have done what she's done."

The lengths Keli went to cover her trail astounded Mr Gillies, who felt deceived by her actions. She organised for the consent forms for the adoption of the first child to be sent by registered mail to Harbord Post Office and then obtained them on Mr Gillies' behalf without his ever knowing. (The court was not told how she managed this.)

For Duncan Gillies there was still very much a burning need to know who the father of all of these children could be. DNA had already cleared him of being the father of the first baby girl born in 1995, and he had moved overseas to the United Kingdom at the time the third child, a boy, was conceived. However it was still possible that he was the father of second baby Tegan, although he certainly didn't believe that was the case.

Duncan Gillies swore that he knew nothing about any of the pregnancies. But the question still remained: how could he not notice his long-term girlfriend was pregnant? And more importantly why didn't Keli tell him? For the two days Mr Gillies was on the stand, the line of questioning must have frequently been both humiliating and embarrassing for him and his wife. Yet to all in the court he appeared to answer every question honestly, he didn't hold back. It was clear that his anger towards Keli had not diminished in any way since learning of her infidelities. Grilled on every minute detail of his life with Keli, and always prepared to answer, in the end the general feeling in the courtroom was that Duncan Gillies was a man who was telling the truth.

a respected family

SILENCE, SECRETS AND SADNESS

chapter **6**

FOR MORE than four long years a petrified Keli Lane kept the police investigation into the disappearance of her second baby, Tegan Lee Lane, a secret. She told none of the people closest in her life – except that is, her husband, the father of her fourth baby, a girl, now three years old. She finally told him in January 2004 – just weeks before their wedding. She told Detective Senior Constable Gaut that she was scared to tell her fiancé because she didn't want to break his heart –and she genuinely feared that her fourth child would be taken from her if the news became public. Breaking the news of her secret past had been hard enough for Keli to tell her shocked but now understanding husband – who seriously considered cancelling their wedding at first – but telling her parents was inconceivable.

For Keli revealing to the mum and dad she respected so much and was so close to, that she had given birth to a baby that had mysteriously disappeared and was now the subject of a massive police investigation, was a daunting prospect.

At the coronial inquest Virginia Fung – Keli's social worker at the time her third baby was born in 1999 – revealed that Keli had told her why she concealed the fact she had a baby in 1995. "She went on to say she had concealed the birth to us because she believed nobody would help her."

Sobbing, Keli explained to Ms Fung that when her parents found out about the first baby – the girl she had given birth to in 1995 when she was just 19 years old and who was adopted – they had angrily disowned her. But it appeared that this might not have been the case. Robert and Sandra Lane claimed they were not aware of the birth of any of the other three babies; they thought they had just the one granddaughter, the fourth baby girl, now three, who Keli and her husband were raising.

Keli would finally admit to the birth of "missing" Tegan to her mum and dad, but still could not bring herself to tell them about the other two babies who had been adopted – that would be up to Detective Senior Constable Gaut. Robert and Sandra Lane would hear about the 1995 and 1999 births from the police officer.

What happened when Keli Lane finally sat her parents down and told them the truth about the police investigation of "missing" baby Tegan will probably never be known. For Keli surely years worth of pent-up emotion must have come flooding to the surface – tears, guilt, sadness, regret, relief even. Did shocked Robert and Sandra Lane react angrily? Were they sympathetic? Did they comfort her and hold her? Or did they chastise her?

For Keli's father it was an especially difficult revelation. As a retired police officer he had spent most of his years on the force serving the community of Manly and now his colleagues were looking into his own daughter's involvement in the possible death of a newborn, her own child.

At the inquest Robert Joseph Arthur Lane, a tall, fit-looking man, explained how he and his wife had been floored when Keli eventually told them about Tegan. "In hindsight I feel a bit foolish," he said, "in that I didn't notice a thing. But I'd had no reason to believe she was pregnant at all."

Dumbfounded already by his daughter's revelation, there was more to come for Robert Lane. Keli had only admitted to the birth of Tegan and it wasn't until Detective Senior Constable Gaut came to speak to Mr and Mrs Lane that they learned the full extent of Keli's deception – they were in fact the grandparents to three children, all of whom they had never met. "He didn't inadvertently say it," explained Mr Lane, who always appeared protective and caring of Keli in court. "But he delicately told us did we know that she had two other children, and that floored us … it was just the shock of knowing that there were additional children that had been adopted out."

"Do you know of any reason why she didn't tell you of those other two?" asked Sergeant Becroft at the inquest.

"I think that she was, right until the end, she wanted to hide it from her family," he answered. Robert Lane felt that Keli had kept the secret to herself because she didn't want to disappoint him and his wife. "She was held in very, very high esteem in the family, and still is," he said. "She was very, very well-known in the community [and] I believe she was trying to hide this episode in her life from everyone because of those pressures."

At the very heart of Keli's deception was always the fear that her parents would disown her – that was evident from what she had told Detective Senior Constable Gaut in her interviews. "Do you feel that if she had disclosed the fact that she was pregnant with any one

At the heart of Keli's deception was always the fear that her parents would disown her. Was that so, the police asked her mother. "Certainly not," Mrs Lane replied fiercely.

of those children, would you have disowned her?" asked Sergeant Becroft. "Certainly not," Mr Lane replied fiercely.

In hindsight Robert Lane said he could see the unhealthy burden Keli carried as a teenager; trying to get to the top of her sport, but at the same time getting her first taste of freedom from her childhood home – and that was when she had fallen pregnant. She was allowed to stay overnight at her boyfriend's house, she had access to a car … it all led to her making poor decisions. "I'd say it was a multitude of circumstances at the time, it was the first time in her life that she had a lot of freedom from our home, not that she was ever held back, but she was constantly in our care, and you know [with the] training and sport we had a very close-knit family, and these things happened, together with other stresses that she was trying to achieve things. I think that it became overbearing and then the thing multiplied and multiplied and multiplied."

Sergeant Becroft was still stunned that Keli's husband and many of her friends hadn't directly questioned her in more detail about the pregnancies, once armed with the shocking facts. Sergeant Becroft remained even more amazed that Keli's parents had simply sat back and accepted what their daughter had told them and not demanded some sort of explanation. "Did you question Keli about the circumstances of those three children?" he was asked. "Not at any great length," Robert Lane shrugged.

"Did you ask her any questions?" Sergeant Becroft persisted. "Yes. Basically (I asked) why she didn't … she knew that we loved her, and we were a close-knit family, there'd be no difficulties that I knew of, or my wife knew of. We wished she'd come to us and she would have got the support from the very start and this thing wouldn't have blossomed or ballooned into the serious thing it is today."

Mr Lane was obviously uncomfortable giving evidence at the inquest – he was more used to being on the other side of the witness box. As a police officer he was used to being the interrogator: he asked the questions, he controlled the conversation. But now here he was on the stand, on the receiving end. And it wasn't only in the glare of the witness box that he felt he was being scrutinised. For the first time in his life, he felt awkward walking down the street to buy a newspaper at the local store. It felt as though everyone was talking about what Keli had done and it was humiliating. His quiet family life had suddenly been snatched from him.

But Robert Lane took his role as Keli's father very seriously. Despite the media attention Mr Lane was determined to stand by his daughter. Each day as Keli struggled through the throng of newspaper reporters, paparazzi and cameramen into the courtroom, we watched Robert Lane hold her hand firmly, walking protectively beside her, always staring straight ahead.

It was a different story with Keli's mother, Sandra Lane, a woman of medium height, with shortish blond hair. She was rarely seen at the inquest. She only attended on the opening day – when she wore a black pant suit similar to the sort Keli often wore, with a cream-coloured skivvy – and when she was called to give evidence. Even then her answers were short and curt. It appeared to those of us reporting on the case that the relationship between mother and daughter was strained. Whereas Keli's father was a familiar sight and an obvious source of strength to Keli, mum Sandra chose to stay away.

Perhaps it was understandable that Mrs Lane would feel awkward facing the assembled court of lawyers, police detectives, social workers and journalists, but when she did arrive on the fourth day of the inquest, her stony gaze had the press bench puzzled. On the stand she rarely glanced in the direction of her daughter, as she tersely described her relationship with Keli as "very good." Mrs Lane said that she had been involved in many of Keli's sporting activities as she grew up, but when she was questioned about their family life she became defensive, saying it was a normal, caring and loving environment.

"If Keli was to come home and say 'Mum, I'm pregnant' how would you have reacted to that?" Sergeant Becroft asked her. "I would have supported her," Mrs Lane said. "Do you think she would have been aware of that?" After a slight pause she replied, "Not necessarily, no."

Mrs Lane admitted that as a woman who had carried two children herself, she found it difficult to accept that she hadn't recognised the signs of pregnancy in her own daughter. She put it down to Keli's work as a PE teacher and the clothes she wore.

"She lived in tracksuits," she explained.

Robert Lane also failed to see the changes in Keli's appearance, but then much like everyone else he wasn't looking for it. "Did you notice any change in her body shape at all?" he was asked. "Well, that varied. At times, well, due to training, water-polo training and physical exercise, if she was doing one sport compared to another sport, so I might have mentally thought 'oh well, Keli's put on a bit of weight' but she was a strong girl and I didn't give it any more thought."

Mr and Mrs Lane trusted Keli as she was growing up. She had never acted wildly or irrationally and had never got in trouble at school or with the law. Even so, her parents were strict about Keli always telling them where she was going. Because the water-polo training facilities were based in Balmain, it was quite usual for Keli not to come home to Fairlight each night; her parents were happy for her to stay with friends in the area or at boyfriend and family friend Duncan Gillies' house – just as long as she told them. But it was now dawning on Robert and Sandra Lane, that much of what their daughter got up to during that period was actually a complete mystery to them.

What has perplexed many people since Keli Lane's case became public is why she didn't have an abortion each time she fell pregnant. To many young girls, abortion would surely have seemed an easier and less painful option. The religious values held by the Lane family may go a small way to explaining Keli's reasons for going full term in each case and actually giving birth. A religious family, the Lanes didn't attend church regularly, but Mrs Lane's personal view was that terminating a pregnancy was wrong. "Would Keli have been aware of your views in relation to terminating a pregnancy?" she was asked. "Quite possibly," said Mrs Lane.

It wasn't that pregnancy was a taboo subject in the Lane household, only that it didn't seem to have any relevance to family life at that time and just wasn't discussed. Sandra Lane had given Keli the normal talks about sex education when she was younger, but they hadn't talked about falling pregnant.

Anyway Keli's mother strongly believed that abortion wouldn't have been an option for Keli. She detailed a conversation her daughter had with both herself and her husband during which she swore to them that she couldn't hurt a baby. "And those were her exact words, she couldn't hurt a baby?" Sergeant Becroft asked Keli's father. "Well, ah, it may not have been her exact words, but she said: 'I couldn't do it Dad. You know I couldn't hurt a baby or hurt children,' or something to that effect."

Mr Lane felt that in some ways he had failed his daughter because she didn't feel she could come to him for help. "She would have got the support from the very start," he said.

However Keli's parents admitted that they were well aware that their daughter was sexually active from 1994, when she was 18. In fact it was her mother who gave her the money for the contraceptive pill. "So by that she didn't conceal the fact that she was having sexual relationships then?" Sandra was asked. "No." – "She felt comfortable to ask you for money for the pill?" – "Yes."

But what was really frustrating Coroner John Abernethy, was that even after being told about their daughter's secret past, Mr and Mrs Lane still didn't quiz Keli as to what had happened to Tegan! It seemed no one in her life was actually prepared to ask any blunt, tough questions. All anyone would tell Mr Abernethy – in response to his frequent requests as to why no one would ask Keli Lane any such direct questions – was that nobody wanted to upset her. That they didn't feel that pushing her to talk about it would help!

Mrs Lane said she had never confronted her daughter because she found it all too upsetting. Her husband felt much the same way. "What did she tell you happened?" Sergeant Becroft asked him. "Well I can't remember having much of a conversation about it because, again we didn't know the seriousness of the matter, and we became detached to some extent because there was a wedding coming up [Keli's wedding] and that was the main objective at the time. It was obviously distressing to my daughter, and I didn't want to create any more traumas to her. And I didn't want to alienate myself and my wife from giving her the support she obviously needed at that time, together with her husband, and particularly the granddaughter, our granddaughter."

Throughout the inquest Coroner Abernethy had participated frequently – asking questions of witnesses himself – although as mentioned, it was his assisting counsel, Sergeant Becroft, who was effectively running the case on a day-to-day basis.

A man who had seen a lot in his time as a coroner, John Abernethy seemed at times as though he had almost lost faith in human kind, perhaps jaded after witnessing so much human cruelty. When he did speak, his strong, booming voice resounded throughout the courtroom. He appeared to frequently become impatient with Keli's family and friends, and their insistence that they had not questioned her about her pregnancies since the scandal became known.

But at the same time he showed great sympathy to Keli herself, as well as frustration.

Generally Mr Abernethy avoided interrupting Sergeant Becroft, although every now and again he couldn't help himself. This was most certainly one of those moments.

He looked on incredulously when Mr Lane said that after speaking to his police buddies at Manly, he had no desire to have daughter Keli further explain her actions. "You never wanted to get to the bottom of it?" he was asked. "No, basically not … because we were detached from it and we didn't know the seriousness of it at the time."

Mrs Lane gave much the same answer, in that she had never felt the need to force Keli to open up. On hearing that, Mr Abernethy interrupted: "Why ever not?"

"Because it's been very distressing," Mrs Lane replied turning in her seat to look directly at the Coroner. "I'm sure it was," he agreed. "I'm sure, but she is your daughter. You can't ask her why she didn't tell you about the pregnancies?"

"I've had a very distressing year with several different things that have happened and when I tried to approach it, I'd get very upset and I felt that it wasn't appropriate to go into an in-depth conversation about it."

The speechless Coroner gave his assisting counsel a shrug of his shoulders, to motion for her to continue questioning the witness.

Sgt. Becroft: "I know this question may be difficult for you but why do you get upset when you think about the whole case?"

Mrs Lane: "Because she was so distressed when she told us about what had happened."

"You still believe that Keli didn't harm Tegan?" her father, retired policeman Robert Lane, was asked. "Of course," he replied confidently. "That Tegan is still alive?" – "I do," he said.

Sgt. Becroft: "You haven't inquired with her why she adopted out baby number one and baby number three?"

Mrs Lane: "Not directly. I assumed that she did that because she wanted them to go to a good home and be looked after well."

Although Mr and Mrs Lane said they believed Keli's story; about giving Tegan to her natural father, they also admitted that it did seem unusual. Keli had told them the same story she had told Detective Senior Constable Gaut: that she had a brief affair with a man who later called her "a whore" and accused her of trying to trap him. Mr Lane winced at the words.

Sgt. Becroft: "Okay, and even the fact that obviously Andrew Norris is in a relationship and that this person Mel accepted to take this child into her home and raise this child, you don't find that that's unusual?"

Mr Lane: "Oh, well, of course it is – this is a most unusual matter, and I think it's unusual. I don't necessarily believe that Andrew Norris or Morris was his correct name, because that's probably not the normal thing for guys to do (when having affairs) outside another partnership, to retain ... their correct name."

The conclusion Mr Lane had come to was that the real father of Tegan was a much older man, who had given Keli a fake name to protect his own identity or to at least hide the relationship from his partner. "I believe the version that Keli has given but I'm not certain of the identity of the people involved," he said.

"And have you actually questioned Keli about this Andrew Norris person, about more specific details?"

Mr Lane said he did ask Keli the age of the man she had slept with and what he looked like, but nothing more than that.

As a retired New South Wales police officer, Mr Lane would also have been well aware of the legal implications of Keli pouring her heart out to him or his wife should a case later come to court. It was perhaps for that reason that his inquiries about the whereabouts of Tegan were minimal. "Overall I think just by her manner she appeared to be quite up front to me and, well, this is the first instance that there's been complications and difficulties in her life [and I believe that has] manifested and snowballed, and she found herself in a difficult situation she couldn't get out of," he said.

Instead Mr Lane avoided asking Keli if she had harmed the child. While he was certain that she had done nothing wrong, he was well aware of the laws in relation to homicide, manslaughter and infanticide. He was certainly not any style of legal guru, but when asked by Sergeant Becroft about his understanding of the law Mr Lane did concede that he had a working knowledge of the legislation.

"You still believe Keli didn't harm Tegan?" he was asked. "Of course," he replied confidently. "That Tegan is still alive?" – "I do."

Throughout the inquest Mr Lane had to listen as the cast of characters in court – nursing staff, social workers and police – repeatedly spoke of the litany of lies that Keli had told. But at the end of the day Keli Lane was still his daughter and he loved her unequivocally. More importantly, he trusted her. The only explanation in Mr Lane's mind as to why Keli would adopt out her other two children and not Tegan, was that she knew the child would go to a good home. "The only thing I could assume from my thoughts would be that she knew who the father was and she may have thought that to get the actual father [to look after her child] might be a bit more beneficial than adoption."

But something did not ring true as each member of the Lane family took the stand. Something was missing, something wasn't right. At no stage did they indicate that Keli didn't have their complete support – indeed, from all accounts the Lane family was very close – yet there still seemed to be so much that they weren't saying.

Despite the explanation for mum Sandra Lane's continued absence from the inquest – she was babysitting Keli's daughter – there was nothing to explain or excuse her iciness when she did attend court; a coldness that seemed directed at everyone, including her own daughter and husband. She was a tough woman to read – she didn't become emotional on the stand as one would expect her to, and she answered Sergeant Becroft's questions with an aloofness that made her appear disconnected and distant. In her defence, she was waking up to see her daughter's face splashed on the front page of every newspaper, switching on the television to see her in frequent news bulletins, hearing her name read out hourly on the radio. Perhaps her cold stare was that of a woman who would do anything to protect her baby girl and who kept her answers as short as possible so as to give nothing away. She simply refused to give those inside the courtroom any insight into the woman she was.

"Have you ever questioned her as to why she didn't tell you about the pregnancies?" asked Sergeant Becroft. "No, I haven't." – "Have you ever stated to her that she may have denied you having contact with your natural grandchildren?" – "No."

Mrs Lane said she had never thought about the fact that she had been denied the opportunity to be the grandmother to a further three children. By way of an explanation for her detachment, she said that her own mother had died just the month before Keli finally revealed the existence of Tegan. Mrs Lane had been incredibly distraught. She felt that it might have been her own grief at that time which stopped Keli telling her the whole story. "It was so difficult to tell me about what had happened at that time [and] she didn't want to upset me more by telling me about the others."

She too believed, as her husband did, that her daughter had been swept off her feet by an older man, a man who had conned and wooed her. Sandra Lane believed that Tegan was now in the care of that man, although she too doubted that his name was Andrew Norris. "Well he could have told her that was his name and it mightn't necessarily be that," she said. Keli's story that Andrew Norris and his girlfriend had taken Tegan into their care seemed strange to Mrs Lane too – the idea that the man's girlfriend was willing to take another woman's child was odd, especially one born from a brief love affair.

But the court needed desperately to establish what had happened to Tegan Lee Lane and the vital clues to her whereabouts lay in the two hours between Keli leaving Auburn Hospital on September 14, 1996 at around 2pm and arriving at Craig and Dianne Hansen's wedding in Manly at 4pm. For Sergeant Becroft it was extremely important that Mrs Lane remember exactly what happened that afternoon.

And Mrs Lane's memory of the wedding day was perfectly clear. She said Keli had rushed in at around 3pm leaving only an hour to get ready for the ceremony. She said her daughter would normally park the car at the end of the driveway or out at the front of the house, but on this particular afternoon she didn't see Keli pull up. She just figured she must have driven, parked somewhere else and walked through the back door gate.

Sgt. Becroft: "How did she seem that day?"
Mrs Lane: "She seemed okay."
Sgt. Becroft: "Not upset?"
Mrs Lane: "No."
Sgt. Becroft: "Just okay? What's that mean?"
Mrs Lane: "Oh just normal."

It was time for Sergeant Becroft to remind the witness, Mrs Lane, that just hours earlier Keli had handed over her newly born baby daughter to someone, knowing that she was going to have very little, or nothing to do with that child for the rest of its life. "Yet she seemed normal?" Sergeant Becroft asked again. "Well, just rushed a little I guess," Mrs Lane replied. "Nothing stood out?" – "Nothing stood out."

Sgt. Becroft: "Pretty cool?"
Mrs Lane: "Well …

Sgt. Becroft: "Wouldn't you think?"

Mrs Lane: "Well, I don't know."

"Put yourself in her position," said Sergeant Becroft. "Imagine having a baby secretly and coming home, getting dressed and going with your boyfriend, and the baby is not his by the way, or we don't think it is – well it might be – and going to a wedding." Mrs Lane was indignant in her reply: "Well, there was a bit of a rush on to get ready."

In the rush to the church it seemed, there was also great confusion. When Keli raced in through the back door of her family house, boyfriend Duncan Gillies was sitting at the kitchen table casually drinking a cup of coffee waiting for her. Keli dashed past him to the shower, promising to be quick. "So Duncan's there having a cup of coffee or something and waiting and Keli came home. You're not sure how she got there but certainly not with Duncan?" Sergeant Becroft asked Mrs Lane. "No, they arrived separately."

Mrs Lane had just given a vital piece of evidence on oath: police were very much looking at the possibility that Keli's boyfriend Duncan Gillies was involved in some way in the disappearance of baby Tegan Lee Lane. Mrs Lane's statement that he was already at the house was very important.

Mrs Lane went on to explain that once Keli was showered, dressed and ready, she had driven the couple to the church herself, dropping them off outside. Then the couple had come back to Fairlight to spend the night when the wedding celebrations were finished.

At the inquest Keli's lawyer Mr Hamill asked Mrs Lane to think very carefully about whether Keli and Duncan had come home together. "Are you also clear in your memory that they came back and stayed the night or are you guessing a little for that?" Mr Hamill asked. "Possibly a guess," Mrs Lane admitted. "But I can't imagine they'd go anywhere else when the wedding was in Manly."

It was time for Coroner Abernethy to interject: "You told me that they stayed the night, which is it? If you don't know say so, you're under oath" he reminded her.

"I don't know for a fact," she answered stiffly.

It was possibly a big ask for anyone to recall specific events from eight years earlier, and as Mrs Lane pointed out, she had no reason to be looking for behaviour that was out of the ordinary. "So it would be fair to say that she may have been quite distressed but that you didn't really pay it any mind?" asked Mr Hamill.

"Well, that's right," said Mrs Lane.

As the court scandal played itself out in Manly, the person who bore much of the brunt of the gossip was Keli's younger brother Morgan. In 1996, when his niece, baby Tegan, disappeared, he was only 18 years old – a typical teenager, hanging out with mates and playing sport. He

Keli's mother's evidence on oath was vital. If her memory of what had happened was correct, Duncan Gillies could not have been involved in baby Tegan's disappearance.

was busy enjoying life and wasn't paying that much attention to what was happening in his sister's world. But when news of the massive investigation into the disappearance of baby Tegan hit the headlines, it was certainly tough and hurtful for Keli's kid brother to hear the vicious rumours that were circulating about his big sis.

It was Robert Lane who broke the news to his son about Keli's pregnancies. Morgan Robbie Lane was 27 years old by the time the matter came before the Coroner, and he told the court he had never broached the subject with Keli, except to occasionally make mention of the emotional impact the case was having on everyone and the unwanted publicity it had attracted.

"I mean it's not a sit down conversation," he explained. "But just like updates as to what's taking place in this process."

Naively Morgan Lane hoped that the media would quickly tire of the story and that he and his family would be free to move on with their lives.

It was for this reason that he didn't want to ask Keli about what had happened, because he believed once the doors closed on the inquest, they could go home and back to living a normal life.

"I realise that once this process finishes that we still have to maintain a relationship. I shouldn't say have to maintain, I want to continue a close relationship with my sister when this all finishes and we still have to live together and we're family."

Openly hostile toward the journalists in the courtroom he fiercely defended his upbringing and described his childhood and teenage years as "second to none". Despite being her junior, Morgan Lane was protective of his older sister and it was his view that the case had had a huge emotional impact on her.

"You never directly asked what happened to Tegan Lane?" asked Sergeant Becroft. "Never wanted to ask," he answered. "It's not as if I blindly believe anything that anyone says. I believe my sister in relation to this. I've seen the mother that she has become, also I've known her my whole life."

Moreover Morgan Lane insisted that he could completely understand why, whoever had baby Tegan – for he too believed that she was still alive – would refuse to come forward. He put it down to fear.

"I can completely understand the motives behind anyone not coming forward," he said, claiming the whole investigation had been poorly handled and as a result his family was at the centre of a media circus.

Like his mother, Keli's brother Morgan found the glare of the court too much to bear and avoided attending unless absolutely necessary; when he was called to give evidence. Still Morgan Lane's absence was less notable than that of Keli's husband, who was also a rare sight at Westmead Coroner's Court. In a bid to quash gossip about her husband's glaring failure to attend the court, Keli's lawyer asked him – on a day he was called – why he didn't attend the court each day with his wife.

"Is it the case that because of the time of the year (June 2005) – that is tick tock, tick tock to the end of the financial year – you're at a particularly busy time at work?" Mr Hamill asked him.

"I would like to be here every day," Keli's husband explained. "But unfortunately I can't." He added that he had asked for the time off work, but it was an impossible time of the year and he had commitments to his employer.

The whole point in calling Keli's family and husband to give evidence, and making them live through the painful facts of Keli's double life all over again – and publicly too – was so that Sergeant Becroft could try to find out if Keli had told them anything of significance as to the whereabouts of Tegan. Or whether the decision by Keli to keep the pregnancies a secret was in any way based on a fear of her family.

But in spite of relentless questioning they all emphatically denied that the talented sportswoman who they called daughter, sister, wife, would have been disowned or ostracised in any way had she asked any one of them for help.

But Sergeant Becroft still suspected that someone close to Keli Lane was hiding the truth and she, along with Detective Senior Constable Gaut, was determined to find out who that person was and what they knew. And in spite of Morgan Lane's naive hopes, the following morning Keli Lane would still be on the front page of the newspapers at the Manly store where his dad liked to shop. Still on screen when his mum switched on the TV.

Tragically for the Lane family, the whole nation was hooked on the case of "missing Tegan Lane".

team players
FAMILY AND FRIENDS CLOSE RANKS

chapter **7**

GROWING UP, playing water-polo meant everything to Keli. In a way it defined who she was. Completely dedicated to the sport, she trained up to four times a week and always with one goal in mind: to make it to the Sydney 2000 Olympic Games. She could think of nothing that would make her prouder than to compete in the sport she adored in front of a huge home crowd, to walk into the stadium and be surrounded by screaming Australian fans, caught up in the Olympic fever that gripped Sydney that year.

Water-polo is the longest-standing team sport in the Olympic Games, although it was only in 1997 that the breakthrough came when women's water-polo was included on the Olympic program. Its debut would be the 2000 Games – held in Keli's hometown, Sydney.

The sport is known as the most physically demanding of all team games. A typical player, just like Keli, is well-built, powerful and able to endure huge exertion – during the hour it takes to complete a game, a player may have covered up to three kilometres in the pool.

The team that Keli played with in her teenage years consisted of a mixed bag. Some of the girls were as committed as she was, while for others it was simply a sport they played and enjoyed, but had no plans to continue with to a professional level.

In 1994 when she was 18 years old, Keli met Stacey Leigh Gaylard. Both were competing at the junior water-polo championships on the Sunshine Coast in Queensland. Stacey was playing in front of her Sunshine Coast home crowd, while Keli had been selected to play for the New South Wales squad.

Bonding during the tournament, the pair became good mates and shortly after the competition Robert and Sandra Lane invited Stacey to come and live at their family home in Fairlight, so she could train with Keli and have the chance to play water-polo in the prestigious, but extremely tough Sydney squad. An excited Stacey jumped at the chance and moved in with the Lanes straight away. She stayed with the family until the end of January 1995, during which time she shared a bedroom with Keli. With the pair training together most week days and going out drinking together at weekends, they soon became close friends. What Stacey was not aware of, though, was that by the time she left the Lane household, water-polo pal 19–year-old Keli was seven months pregnant with her first child.

On June 27, 2005 Ms Gaylard was called to give evidence at the inquest. She explained to the Coroner that in the months she was living with Keli she had never seen her naked or even get changed. "Well, we usually weren't in the same room at the same time getting undressed," she explained. "[It was like] if one of us would be in then one of us would be out, we'd be getting ready for training, so it wasn't like we were in the same room all the time, I can't recall ever being in the same room when we were changing."

A couple of Keli's water polo team-mates suspected that she might be pregnant. So they donned their goggles and dived into the pool to make a closer inspection!

Sergeant Becroft wanted to know if Ms Gaylard had noticed anything unusual in Keli's behaviour while she was living with her. Stacey Gaylard thought about the question for a while. "No," she eventually replied. "It wasn't unusual."

Keli played water-polo for the entire duration of her first pregnancy. At no stage did any of her team mates suspect that she was pregnant, although there had been whispers about her weight. The second pregnancy, though, was different. Some of the girls started to notice Keli's odd behaviour. At training the girls had become accustomed to walking around in their swimsuits, so it seemed somewhat strange when Keli suddenly started covering up.

It was some time during the first half of 1996 that Ms Gaylard discussed Keli's sudden weight gain around her stomach area with another player Tarryn Woods – who happened to be the girl Keli's boyfriend Duncan Gillies had slept with early on in their relationship after a surf club carnival. Knowing that the water-polo circle was small, Duncan Gillies had confessed his one-night stand to Keli. A petite blonde, Tarryn was just as aggressive as Keli in the pool – sadly for Keli, Tarryn would go on to live her friend's dream and represent Australia as part of the women's water-polo squad at the Sydney 2000 Olympic Games where the team won Gold.

Both housemate Stacey and love rival Tarryn had suspicions that Keli was pregnant. They had noted that she seemed self-conscious and had taken to wearing tracksuits all the time, regardless of the weather. Whenever she was poolside she would wear a towel wrapped tightly under her arms and would only drop it on the edge of the pool just before quickly slipping into the water.

Ms Gaylard remembered thinking that Keli's torso looked massive and said as much to Tarryn Woods. They decided to investigate and figured their best bet would be to take a look underwater! So they donned their goggles and dived in for a closer inspection.

Sgt. Becroft: "Did you and Tarryn then speak about that?"
Ms Gaylard: "We confirmed our suspicions to each other."
Sgt. Becroft: "What did you say to each other?"
Ms Gaylard: "She looks like she is pregnant."
Sgt. Becroft: "Was that the end of the conversation?"
Ms Gaylard: "That was the end of it, we never spoke about it again."

To Sergeant Becroft it seemed unusual that the young girls would suspect that their friend was pregnant and then not talk or gossip about it – either between themselves or with their other girlfriends. And most of all why on earth didn't they bring it up directly with Keli?

Sgt. Becroft: "When you were in the swimming pool and you put your goggles on and you swam under the water and you basically identified what you believed, that Keli was pregnant, did you mention that to her at any time?"
Ms Gaylard: "No."
Sgt. Becroft: "Do you recall seeing Keli not pregnant after that time?"

Ms Gaylard: "I can't remember because I stopped playing at the end of 1996."

But that didn't mean that Stacey Gaylard had stopped thinking about her friend, wondering what she would do about the pregnancy. She could see that Keli had made up her mind to go ahead with the birth, which in itself seemed to be a surprising decision – everyone in their circle of friends was well aware of Keli Lane's passionate desire to play water-polo for Australia. Giving birth would surely put a quick end to that dream.

That aside, Ms Gaylard assumed – it seemed logical to her – that Keli's boyfriend Duncan Gillies knew about the pregnancy, based on her assumption that he was the baby's father. How wrong she was.

After the initial underwater investigation by the inquisitive two girls, Stacey Gaylard hadn't thought much more about her pregnant pal, until, out of the blue, it suddenly occurred to her one day, that her mate must have given birth. But even that random thought didn't trigger an urge to make contact with her friend.

Sgt. Becroft: "Did you turn your mind to wonder what she did to the child, with the child, after you saw her?"
Ms Gaylard: "No, I didn't really think about it."
Sgt. Becroft: "You didn't ask her?"
Ms Gaylard: "No."

It was difficult for Sergeant Becroft to believe that a lively teen like Stacey Gaylard had not pursued her shocking discovery, but since the witness was under oath, she had no choice other than to accept that what she was hearing was the truth.

However Ms Gaylard did tell the assisting counsel that she believed Tarryn's father David Woods knew that one of his star players was pregnant. Mr Woods was at that time coaching the Balmain women's water-polo team of which all three girls were members.

Sgt. Becroft: "Tarryn never told you that she'd spoken to her father about it?"
Ms Gaylard: "No."

But Ms Gaylard was still quite sure that the coach was aware of what was going on.

Sgt. Becroft: "What makes you think that?"

Ms Gaylard: "Because Mr Woods is a father of three children. If we, as the girls on the side of pool noticed it, he would have had to have noticed it as well because we're in the water playing; he was standing on the edge. So I think it would have been very hard for him to have missed it."

Sgt. Becroft: "Are you aware of Tarryn's father Dave Woods ever mentioning Keli being pregnant to Keli herself?"

Ms Gaylard: "No."

Swim coach David Woods was called to the stand on June 28, 2005. A fit-looking man in his early sixties, he told the court that he would often host barbecues after the girls' games and Keli was nearly always there, because she was one of the most sociable girls on the team. Mr Woods said he remembered Keli as a tough competitor who was an absolute pleasure to coach and who always appeared to be having a good time hanging out with her team mates.

Mr Woods said he was just as shocked as everyone else when he heard the news about the three births and the missing child. He did admit though that he had thought Keli Lane was pregnant around mid-1996 (when Keli was carrying baby Tegan), as there had been speculation amongst some of the girls. But he didn't feel it was his place to mention it. "Well being the coach of a women's water-polo team, or any women's sport, it's a bit of a knife-edged thing," he explained. "Talking about pregnancy with an 18- or 19-year-old, it's not a good place to go."

Sergeant Becroft wanted to know if the rumours were persistent or just something that he had heard in passing. "It wasn't persistent," he said. "It was mentioned a few times and I just kind of thought if she was pregnant, probably her mother wouldn't let her play or I didn't think it was an issue."

Perhaps proof of her dedication to the sport, Keli played in the water-polo grand final in March 1995, which was the same month she gave birth to her first daughter. "I found this surprising because

I recall that Keli played in the final that year, and she played well." Mr Woods said that her performance had stunned him because "she looked overweight and I didn't expect her to play well."

Just four months later Keli flew to Quebec in Canada to represent Australia in the water-polo junior world championships. It was her zenith. It was here she would play the match of her life. Already considered a great water-polo talent, she wowed the crowd as she scored twice in a semi-final win over the United States. She then went on to play versus Holland in the final, but unfortunately the Australian team lost. One of Keli's team mates on that trip observed to *The Daily Telegraph* on October 29, 2004 that Keli was not that close to the other team members. "Keli was always considered a bit of an outsider," she said, "because she did not come through the usual Australian Institute of Sport channels."

Admired by coach David Woods for her aggression in the pool, Keli did not command the same respect from his daughter Tarryn, who had a less than warm relationship with Keli. Understandably the friendship between the girls appeared to have cooled off after Tarryn slept with Keli's boyfriend Duncan Gillies. It was that indiscretion which we on the press bench believed to be the reason Ms Woods had refused to give a statement to the police when they first approached her. In the end the Coroner threatened to issue a subpoena to force her to attend. She did so – of her own free will – in the final week of the inquest on February 13, 2006.

And so it was with bated breath that we watched as a blonde, athletic and slim although broad-shouldered Tarryn Woods arrived at the Coroner's Court. We were all anxious to see how the pair would face off. Would there would be any animosity between them? Everyone was aware of Tarryn's one–night stand with Keli's boyfriend Duncan Gillies, but would it be mentioned in court? After being sworn in, Ms Woods wasted no time in describing Keli as a "really lovely, friendly, happy person." She said they were good friends throughout their water-polo days, but she was also quick to stress that they were not close enough mates to discuss the personal, intimate details of their lives – they were just "normal girlfriends".

But sitting in the courtroom that day and witnessing Tarryn Woods say those words first hand, it was hard to believe everything Ms Woods was saying. The tone of her voice was far from convincing and she was obviously angry that she had been forced to give evidence. It just didn't sound as though she really meant what she was saying. It was understandable that she didn't enjoy the experience of being summonsed to court to give evidence in such a high-profile scandalous matter – by now Tarryn Woods herself was a high profile sportswoman, who spent much of her time competing overseas. How could she have known that a teenage indiscretion – a one-night fling – which happened years earlier, would play out like this; broadcast across the nation's media? She must have felt some resentment that her upstanding reputation was being sullied.

The reason she had refused to give a statement to police, Ms Woods said, was because she felt she had nothing useful to say, nothing that would in any way help the case. She was adamant that it was not because she had anything to hide, or knew something that she wanted to keep from the investigating officers.

She said it was impossible for her to come forward in 2005 because she had been overseas competing in Italy. "I was overseas when all of this happened [and] I didn't think I had anything to offer so didn't make an early statement, and then when I eventually did, I [felt] that

Everyone in the courtroom was aware that the witness had had a one-night stand with Keli's boyfriend. How would the pair face off now she was about to give evidence?

the police [believed] I was hiding something, or you know, had been telling untruths, which wasn't the case."

Tarryn Woods explained that the decision to don goggles and check out Keli's stomach had been a spur of the moment thing.

"Well, I guess it was more noticing [Keli's] weight gain and, you know, as you look at everybody under the water through your goggles, and I guess you know there was the question in our mind that that was a possibility." She said she and Stacey Gaylard weren't the only ones to notice Keli's weight gain – a lot of their friends had been whispering that perhaps Keli was pregnant, but from memory no one said anything to Keli.

Sgt. Becroft: "Why wouldn't you have told her about these rumours or ask her if she was pregnant?"

Ms Woods: "I guess it's hard to say. As a friend – weight gain at a young age is a very delicate issue and certainly while her weight gain may have suggested she might have been pregnant she certainly – you know – she was still playing water-polo and those sorts of things. So I assumed that it probably wasn't the case."

AS THE INQUEST progressed, it became increasingly obvious that a number of Keli's friends had suspected she was pregnant. Melinda Ward became friends with Keli when they were both in primary school and they played water-polo together for about 10 years, although Melinda was never as serious as Keli about the sport. She recalled that in 1995 or 1996 there was a lot of talk about Keli possibly having had a baby. But she said the gossip was more sly comments from the boys on the sidelines than remarks from the girls in the pool. "Thinking [back] now she did just look like she'd put on weight," said Ms Ward, "rather than just having a round stomach like a typical pregnancy."

Melinda Ward didn't notice any change in Keli's body shape during the other pregnancies. "I think because we were playing water-polo [at that time]," she said, "and I saw her in the costume rather than just sort of in clothes." She distinctly remembered the vicious gossip, but believed there was no truth in what was being spread – if she had suspected it was true she would have mentioned it to Keli. Melinda's then boyfriend Brandon Ward, who she later married, also remembered Keli piling on the kilos in 1995. "Geez, Kel's put on a bit of weight" he recalled saying, but only to a couple of his male friends. "It's not really mentioned to the girls," he explained at the inquest. "Because obviously girls are fairly – you know – touchy about their weight. Just typical boy banter," he added. "Same as if a bloke goes overseas and comes back [and had] put on a bit of weight and you say 'Geez, you look like you've swallowed a sheep!'" Not surprisingly, no one ever said that to Keli. Both Brandon and Melinda Ward socialised with Keli, although they didn't see much of her outside the water-polo

season. Keli tended to spend that period largely at Duncan Gilles'
house in Gladesville. During the season, though, they would all head
out together after a game – normally it would be in Manly somewhere,
although occasionally they hit the Balmain pubs. The hotel they would
visit would often depend on which establishment was sponsoring the
team at that time. Brandon remembered that at one stage it was The
Bridge Hotel in Rozelle and for a number of years it was the Town Hall
Hotel in Balmain, which was the sponsor around the time of Keli's
second pregnancy in 1996.

Sgt. Becroft: "When you were at the Town Hall Hotel, out socialising with
Keli, did you ever see her being flirtatious towards other men?"
Mr Ward: "Not off the top of my head, no."

Brandon Ward held Keli in high regard and said she wasn't the type
of girl to have an affair. In all the years that they had been hitting the
pub scene together, Keli had never "played the room". She was happy
just hanging out with her mates. Brandon's wife Melinda agreed.

Sgt. Becroft: "Do you recall her being friendly or talkative to a man
whilst at the Town Hall Hotel with the name perhaps Andrew, or
surname of Norris?"
Mrs Ward: "No."
Coroner John Abernethy: "Or any man other than Duncan Gillies?"
Mrs Ward: "Just people that we played water–polo with on a friendly
basis."
Coroner John Abernethy: "But no one in particular?"
Mrs Ward: "No."

The first time the subject of Keli's secret births was raised in
conversation with Melinda and Brandon Ward was November 5, 2003,
at the couple's Harbord home.

Melinda invited Keli over for a cup of coffee after netball practice.
The three friends were sitting in the lounge room, when it was
mentioned that Detective Senior Constable Gaut had called Melinda. It
was obvious that Keli felt uncomfortable and she quickly put a stop to
the conversation, saying it was something that had happened a long

time ago and it involved her ex-boyfriend Duncan, his brother Simon and his wife Narelle.

"I think she was quite shocked," said Melinda Ward, "that we had been informed and it was just something that came out. She didn't want to pursue the conversation or add to the conversation, so we just left it as that was the answer and I haven't spoken to her about it since."

Brandon Ward told the Coroner that from his recollection Keli had said curtly: "It's got nothing to do with you. It's between Duncan, Narelle and Simon." he went on to explain, "That was that ... that was the whole conversation. We just said, 'Look, fair enough. We just thought we'd let you know,' because to be totally honest the detective had rung us time and time and time again to the point where it was actually, 'God, what more can we tell you? We don't know!'

"You know when you don't know something you don't know, but he kept ringing us."

Increasingly agitated by this unwelcome interference in their lives, Brandon Ward eventually agreed to make a statement to police – he

Time and time again the police detective rang Keli's friends to ask about her. "God, what more can we tell you?" one witness said in desperation. "We don't know!"

claimed Detective Senior Constable Gaut had told them that if they did so, that would be the end of it. "I don't doubt," sympathised the Coroner, "and you've become very important to the whole process. But I'm afraid we've got to subvert our own impatience about these matters to the greater good. We're just trying to find out what happened to the child. You understand that surely?"

"I do understand it," Mr Ward replied. "But you know there is a point where it does start to affect your family. I'd love this thing to be resolved and you know we can all get on and [for] everything to work out really well."

During a 2004 interview with Keli, Detective Senior Constable Gaut asked her: "I'm interested why those three names (Duncan, Simon and Narelle) have come up. What's it got to do with them?" he asked. "Well, I guess they're involved too," replied Keli "because I was going out with Duncan." Keli said that Simon and Narelle had lived around the corner from Duncan; that they all spent a lot of time together. However, she insisted they knew nothing about the pregnancies. Keli claimed she only told Brandon and Melinda that Simon and Narelle were involved to protect them, as they were her friends – "to calm them, to just tell them not to worry because they're people they know," she explained. "They don't know Andrew; they don't know anything about that. I didn't want them to feel obligated to be involved."

"Just to clear it up," said Detective Senior Constable Gaut. "Are you saying that it's got nothing to do with anyone, you just picked those names out basically to put them off the track?" – "Not put them off the track, to make them feel that they don't need to be involved."

"Just hear me out," continued Detective Senior Constable Gaut. "Do you say those three names so people wouldn't be talking about you behind your back as in, 'What's she done with the baby? That maybe she's given it to Narelle and Simon.' Is that something to quash the rumours?" Keli said she had been unhappy about Detective Senior Constable Gaut telephoning her friends to ask about the pregnancies.

"I didn't realise you had spoken to everyone," she huffed. "I didn't realise that it was common knowledge. I just said Duncan, Simon and Narelle because Brandon and Melinda know all three of them."

Consistent in their devotion and loyalty to Keli Lane, good friends Brandon and Melinda Ward have stood by Keli throughout the whole "missing baby" saga. They were both genuinely elated when they read in the newspapers that police believed they had found Tegan Lane (who turned out to be Teagan Chapman) in Queensland.

"I had my fingers crossed," said Brandon Ward. "You know (when) that thing in the paper came up the other day. Melinda and I were so happy and thought it's finally [over], everything's been resolved. You know we had our fingers crossed and everything. Unfortunately it didn't work out that way."

"We're quite protective of Keli," he added. "In the fact that she's one of our closest friends but in saying that, the truth does have to come out and you know we've told you everything we possibly know."

A visibly moved Keli Lane became quite teary on hearing the thoughtful words of her friends. On a Tuesday each week she looked after their two children, who at that stage were aged three years and eleven months, and knowing she had their undivided support obviously meant a lot to her. "She's sensational with them," said Brandon of Keli's time with his two children. "She's caring, she's generous, and I've got no problem whatsoever, she's like an awesome person. Trustworthy, generous, just a great person. Just a – you know – good friend." It was even harder hearing it from Melinda who had been her friend for 25 years. "She's wonderful," Melinda said looking at Keli. "The kids love her and she loves them. They have a great time."

The Wards said they had seen Keli interact with newborn babies on many occasions and were adamant that she wouldn't have hurt an infant. "She loves them," gushed Melinda. "She's great with them, she's always willing to hold babies and she's really receptive to them."

It was obviously incredibly difficult for the couple to face the court, especially since they too were in the dark as to the whereabouts of baby Tegan. Even so, their faith in Keli was noticeably unwavering. "She's a loving, caring person who would stick by you, a really good friend," said Melinda Ward. "She's been my friend since I can remember. She's always been there for me and she's a great girl."

Another devoted friend who stood by Keli was actress Allison Gaye Cratchley, who starred in the Nine Network drama series *Water Rats* and currently plays Dr Zoe Gallagher on *All Saints* on Network Seven. Allison remembered the horrible rumours circulating in 1995 and 1996. "There were rumours," she told the Coroner. "However Manly can be a very toxic place, and if you put on a little bit of weight, next thing you're accused of being pregnant and that is something that's happened to me in the past. So I dismissed that as just rumours."

Ms Cratchley admitted that she had talked about Keli's weight gain with other girlfriends, but said the conversation was more about how nasty the boys were being, rather than any malicious gossip on their behalf. In her statement to the police she said that she had never considered bringing it up with Keli because she "had a lot going on in her (own) life."

Allison Cratchley's friendship with Keli stemmed from the Manly social scene, rather than water-polo. "I always looked at her like a younger sister in our friendship, our time together," she told the Coroner. "She was always a happy, a very happy-go-lucky, a very enthusiastic person who really took life on with a lot of gusto, and I even know that my sister did water-polo with her and absolutely adored her."

There was one particular night, though, which did stand out in the mind of the popular actress. One evening when about 20 of their friends were all hanging out at the Skiff Club in Manly together, someone referred to the pregnancy.

"Someone said 'you know that she went north with her mother' and I just didn't think that that would be true."

Allison Cratchley's feeling was that Keli wasn't particularly close to her mother, so the idea that Keli would have done what was being suggested sounded absurd.

"I just thought it was silly, that that would happen."

Keli Lane had a couple of boyfriends growing up, Ms Cratchley observed, but no more than any of the others girls they were hanging around with. She said Keli was a bit of a "social butterfly" and when she was single she enjoyed male attention.

"You know it's just one of those things where when you're not dating someone you go out and you might get a kiss here or a kiss there [but] it wouldn't be anything serious or anything like that. It would just be more about, you now, meeting someone and just having a kiss but I wouldn't think of anything else." She was quick to stress that Keli wasn't promiscuous. "Keli never really went off into any corner, dark corner or anything like that," she said. "She was always, you know, always fun and good to have a chat with."

Sgt. Becroft: "Did you ever see her going home at the end of the night with another man to, if I could use the term, [have] a one-night stand?"

Ms Cratchley: "No, not at all."

It was the same reply from all of Keli's friends. Not one of them thought of Keli as a "good-time girl". She was more the sort who preferred to spend time with her friends, talking and having a few drinks. Stacey Gaylard and Tarryn Woods were both adamant that Keli didn't sleep around, although it was no secret that she liked to enjoy herself. "We'd usually meet the Wests water-polo boys (Wests Water-Polo Magpies club at Ashfield) there and then most of the girls would hang out with them," Tarryn said. "I didn't see Keli socialising with anybody else but I don't know whether I really took any notice of whether she was talking to anybody else."

Keli often stayed at Tarryn's house after a big night out drinking in Balmain as it was closer than travelling home to her parents place in Fairlight or boyfriend Duncan's in Gladesville. A lot of the girls would crash on the floor in the Woods's lounge room. With so many people heading back to her house, Tarryn accepted that it would have been easy for one of them to have gone missing and for it to have gone unnoticed – although she thought if Keli had wandered off in the pub for an extended time, to talk to a man they didn't know, it would definitely have been brought up.

Sgt. Becroft: "Do you recall any time Keli perhaps breaking off from the group and going and speaking to another male person?"

Ms Woods: "Not anyone specifically that I can recall. She may have spoken to other people at the pub but no one that I noticed."

At that time in their life, when all the girls were in their late teens and early twenties, the partying was frequent and often heavy. Keli loved to have a few drinks and would often become intoxicated, as they all did, and according to her friends sometimes that ended with her going home on the arm of someone she had only just met.

Sgt. Becroft: "Are you aware of Keli ever having any one night stands, going home with a male after being out with the group?"

Ms Woods: "I don't know of a specific one, but I know that it would have happened."

Sgt. Becroft: "But you don't know who with?"

Ms Woods: "No."

Sgt. Becroft: "Was there any occasion when Keli was supposed to sleep at your house and didn't end up going home with you that night?"

Ms Woods: "Not that I recall. There were lots of people staying and whatever so I don't – not that I recall."

Through her line of questioning Sergeant Becroft was trying to establish whether any of the water-polo players had come across Andrew Norris. But she received the same answer from all of them – "No!" Tarryn had never heard his name mentioned – although co-incidentally the address Keli gave to police as Andrew Norris's was a street that was on the walk home from the Town Hall Hotel to Tarryn's house.

The Balmain scene was really the girls' territory. It was rare that Duncan would venture out on that side of the city. If Keli was planning to meet up with him, she would always drive to Manly, where he would be drinking with his rugby buddies. Tarryn did remember an occasion though in August 1996, a month before Tegan was born, when Keli brought Duncan to her 21st birthday in Balmain. From what she could remember Keli was drinking that night and the three of them had a general discussion about relationships. Tarryn was certain that there was no Andrew Norris at that party.

Over the years Tarryn and Keli lost contact with each other as their lives headed off in different directions. But they did have lunch together in April 2005, which was shortly before the inquest started. One of their mutual friends had organised a get-together in Manly and both were guests at the do. Tarryn said that every person at the table was aware of the Tegan "missing baby" scandal, but in friend Keli's presence, they made a point of steering clear of the subject. "Not a word?" asked the Coroner incredulously.

But all Keli's friends had the same answer – No, not a word!

who and where is andrew norris?

NOW THAT Duncan Gillies, Keli Lane's boyfriend from 1994 until 1998, had been ruled out as being the father of missing baby Tegan, the second daughter she gave birth to in 1996 – or at least by this stage police were pretty sure he wasn't involved – they turned their attention to the man Keli kept insisting was the child's father: the mysterious Andrew Norris. She claimed he had fathered baby Tegan following a short-lived fling, but so far had failed to come up with the mobile phone number she said she had for him.

Keli's physical description of Andrew Norris did not help a great deal either. In her interview with Detective Senior Constable Gaut in May 2003, she had explained that Andrew would now be about 37 years old and that he was good looking, Caucasian, about 178cm (5ft 11in), with sun-bleached light brown/blond hair, a tanned complexion, well-built and he possibly went to The University of Sydney. She could have been describing any stereotypical Aussie male!

According to Keli when she met Andrew in late 1995, he was working in the city – in finance or banking – and was living in the Balmain area. Probably the most significant piece of information was that he had been living with his long-term girlfriend Mel, but she was out of town for a few days when he and Keli had first met.

To Detective Senior Constable Gaut, Andrew sounded like an all-round scoundrel – cheating on his partner while she was away, with a girl he had only just met at the pub and sleeping with her in the couple's bed.

Although Keli said she was on the contraceptive pill, it hadn't exactly proved to be an effective method over the years – all four of her children were conceived while she claimed she was taking it. If Keli's story were true, that meant she and Andrew had only relied on the pill for protection when having sex. Andrew didn't wear a condom

– which in itself was putting them both at risk of contracting a sexually transmittable disease.

But much of what Keli had told police and social workers about Tegan's father had been erroneous. Indeed Andrew Norris was the second man she claimed to be the father. First of all she claimed it was Duncan Gillies and now the elusive Andrew Norris. During the 2003 police interview Detective Senior Constable Gaut tried to break through Keli's lies, pleading with her to tell the truth. "The problem is the information you've given me about him I don't believe is true. I believe we could clear this matter up today if you would tell us the truth. I don't believe you've told me the truth so far."

According to Keli, when she finally told the mysterious Andrew Norris she was pregnant he was furious. "He said that I'd trapped him, and that I was a slut," she told the police.

Keli said she had only known Andrew Norris for a matter of weeks when she fell pregnant with Tegan, although she was never sure of the exact date that the baby was conceived. It wasn't until 12 to 14 weeks into the pregnancy that she feared she might be expecting again, she said. Keli had been to the doctor who had confirmed she was pregnant, but it was a further two to three weeks before she could summon the courage to break the news to Andrew. "He was very rude and aggressive," she told Detective Senior Constable Gaut. "And not pleased … he said that I'd trapped him, and that I was a slut." The pregnancy spelt the end of the pair's brief association, she said. By then Keli had been in a relationship with Duncan Gillies for close to two years and was spending many of her nights at his home, but she says she never felt the need to confess to the affair. Detective Senior Constable Gaut wanted to know how she was so sure that Andrew Norris was in fact the father and not her boyfriend, Duncan Gillies.

Det. Sen. Con. Gaut: "When you fell pregnant was it a case that you knew that there's no …"

Ms Lane: "Oh, yeah, there was no way it was Duncan."

Det. Sen. Con. Gaut: "And that's because you hadn't had sex with him for some period around that time?"

Ms Lane: "Yeah."

Andrew Norris pretty much cut all contact with Keli after learning that she was having his child, claimed Keli. "So was there any contact between the time that you found out you were pregnant and told him and when you went to hospital?" asked Detective Senior Constable Gaut. In spite of his many hours of questioning Keli, the determined detective never ceased to be surprised by her unexpected answers and elaborate explanations, and this was one of those times. Keli explained to him during the 2004 interview that in the early stages of the pregnancy they (she and Andrew Norris) had never discussed what would happen to the child. The conversation during which Andrew agreed to take care of Tegan had only taken place the day after Tegan was born when Andrew visited her in the hospital.

Det. Sen. Con. Gaut: "Were they planning to take her home prior to that? Was the plan for them to take her home prior to that?"

Ms Lane: "He didn't trust that I was going to. It wasn't definite, but I said that I wasn't able to keep her and he said they were willing to take her. But I thought after I had her I'd be able to keep her."

(Listening to the videotaped recording of Keli's interview with Detective Senior Constable Gaut being replayed in court, I remember being stunned when I heard Keli say that she had considered keeping Tegan. Until that point there had been no mention of her wanting to keep any of the three children that she gave away and it gave another insight into the woman who had intrigued me for so many months now. I had always believed that she had been desperate to get Tegan out of her life, so this one comment to the detective shed a whole new light on the disappearance – it suggested that Keli had struggled with her decision.)

Unsure as to whether Andrew Norris even existed – and suspecting he didn't – Detective Senior Constable Gaut told Keli that the only way he could determine the truth was to speak to her friends. But Keli became distraught: "Because I don't know where he is, everybody's lives are going to be destroyed? Because I can't get into contact with someone I barely know? He told me not to contact him, I don't have anything else to say. I'm not sure what to say."

It had been a tearful Keli who had explained to social worker Ms Alicia Baltra-Vasquez at Auburn Hospital in 1996, when Tegan was born, that she was all alone and had no one to support her – her boyfriend (Duncan Gillies) was overseas and her parents lived in Perth, she'd said.

With Duncan Gillies listed as the father of all three of her children it wasn't until her interview with Detective Senior Constable Kehoe in February 2001 that she even whispered the name Andrew "Morris" (whose surname she would later say she had given as Norris) claiming he had visited her in hospital. Detective Senior Constable Gaut was quick to tackle Keli on those discrepancies.

Det. Sen. Con. Gaut: "If Andrew was coming and his wife was coming, why would you tell a social worker a story that would suggest that you don't have any friends, or anyone that's going to visit you in hospital while you're there?"

Ms Lane: "Well, he only came to make sure that I was okay, and that the baby was okay."

Det. Sen. Con. Gaut: "Why would you make up that sort of story if you knew that Andrew and his girlfriend were going to come and pick [up] the baby from there?"

Ms Lane: "Because I knew that they were just coming to get Tegan, they didn't care about me. They're not interested in how I was in the end, it wasn't like we were all friends. They didn't give me any support."

But Keli Lane's elaborate stories were getting harder and harder to fathom – indeed even for those of us really close to the case, covering it every day, keeping abreast of the latest information, the new twists and turns were becoming increasingly difficult.

Of course Keli had told kindly Anglicare Adoption Agency social worker Virginia Fung a completely different version of events in 1999, when Ms Fung was dealing with the adoption of her third child, a baby boy. Ms Fung, along with other child protection workers, had by now discovered the truth – that the 1999 pregnancy was not Keli's first as she had pretended. Ms Fung had built up a trusting relationship with Keli nevertheless; probably the only professional to ever get near to the troubled young woman.

It was in that spirit of trust that Keli sent Ms Fung a fax saying she had given her second baby, born in 1996, to a Perth couple, who had befriended her shortly before the birth. Tegan, she said, was living with them, although she explained she had no way of reaching them. *"I know somehow that you know I am being honest with you ... I am being honest with you,"* wrote Keli.

When Detective Senior Constable Gaut asked her for more details Keli said that the Perth couple was actually Andrew and Mel. But he just wasn't buying that – it seemed to him that the letter implied the Perth couple was relatively unknown to Keli.

"I didn't just give her away to anybody," cried Keli clearly distressed. "That's what you're trying to say that says and it doesn't [mean that]."

Keli explained that the relationship she had with Andrew was extremely tense and that Mel hated her.

"Was she happy to take the child?" Detective Senior Constable Gaut asked.

"I think so," replied Keli.

"Do you find that odd?"

"I'm not sure what their relationship was like, I'm not sure what they talked about, but I would find that odd, yes," replied Keli.

She added that before Mel came to the hospital, they had never spoken. All she knew about Mel was that she was Andrew's girlfriend, "I knew of her previously," she said. "But she didn't know about Andrew and I."

For much of her first interview with Detective Senior Constable Gaut in May 2003, Keli was evasive and non-committal. After all, in all the time the police had been searching for Andrew Norris, she had never mentioned the possibility that he could be living in Perth. "I'm not sure what his plans were," she tried to explain. "He wasn't going to tell me. Some of the conversations I had with Andrew indicated perhaps he wasn't going to stay in Sydney because of the embarrassment that I'd caused him, or could cause him."

"Did he ever say he was going to Perth?" asked Detective Senior Constable Gaut.

"Not directly, he just said something along the lines of 'I don't know how I can stay in Sydney, what will everyone think? It's such an embarrassment'."

Quick-minded Detective Senior Constable Gaut then cross-referenced a claim from Keli that she had nothing to do with Andrew for the duration of the pregnancy, with another claim she had earlier made to Detective Senior Constable Kehoe. She had said that Andrew had celebrated his 30th birthday in the July or August of 1996 at the Town Hall Hotel, which would have been when Keli was seven or eight months pregnant. Yet she had claimed they were not speaking!

"How do you want me to explain this?" she asked. "They were there and we were kind of there, and he knew I was there, I knew he was there. I couldn't very well go up and make a show when all these people didn't even know who I was." In other words Keli was saying that she hadn't been invited to Andrew Norris' 30th birthday party; it was just sheer coincidence that she happened to be drinking at the same pub on the same night.

Detective Senior Constable Gaut decided that his best chance of finding Andrew Norris was to make a request to each state and territory's Department of Births, Deaths and Marriages to check their records. He was taking no chances that the information Keli had provided him with was true regarding Andrew's birth date, so he decided to widen the search to include all men of that name who were born between 1960 and 1976. The search came up with a list of 37 men.

With the names in his hand, Detective Senior Constable Gaut began the arduous task of contacting each Andrew Norris individually. He told the Coroner that he personally made hundreds of telephone calls in his bid to hunt down the elusive Andrew Norris. It didn't take long to rule out 24 of the men after they had made statements to police. Either they weren't in the country at the time Tegan was conceived or born, or they had never lived in the Balmain area. The other 13 men were more difficult to track down, so police accessed their personal files and from those details were able to rule out a further nine.

That left just four men whom police couldn't trace and bizarrely one of those happened to be a criminal, who had simply used the name Andrew Norris as an alias for one of his many criminal activities! At the inquest Keli's lawyer Peter Hamill questioned Detective Senior Constable Gaut about his search.

"I'm not being critical at all because you've contacted a lot of Andrew Norrises but was there any particular reason you couldn't contact the other four?" asked Keli's lawyer. "Yes," Detective Senior Constable Gaut replied "I couldn't find addresses for them."

While it was becoming increasingly obvious to Detective Senior Constable Gaut that Andrew Norris was a fictional character, he doggedly continued making inquiries. He phoned the Australian Taxation Office and the Roads and Traffic Authority to try and find addresses for the remaining four Andrew Norrises, yet came up with nothing of any relevance.

"We've done police computer checks for both names, Andrew Morris and Andrew Norris, born around 1966," Detective Senior Constable Gaut told Keli. "And we've been unable to find any person who could be the father of your child through that avenue."

Another clue Keli had offered was that Andrew had studied at The University of Sydney. Detective Senior Constable Gaut wasn't overly surprised when he telephoned The University of Sydney and was informed that the institution had no record of any Andrew Norris or Morris having attended classes around the time Keli indicated. What's more, they added, in case it helped, they had no person by that name on file who was born between 1960 and 1970 having ever enrolled there. "We weren't able to locate him that way," said Detective Senior Constable Gaut, exasperated. "You've told us that you believed he was a student there. They've got no records of him."

While Detective Senior Constable Gaut scoured electoral roles and the electronic White Pages and issued media releases with photographs of Keli from 1996 (with the idea that someone might remember her being pregnant, or have information that could help with the investigation), Keli was conducting her own secret search for the father. Three weeks after the case became public, she posted a message on the website *schoolfriends.com.au* under the title "Andrew Norris". Dated November 18, 2004 it said: *"Looking for Andrew Norris. Age approx. 38. Went to school possibly in western Sydney, Went on to university then entered stock broking/money markets."*

When she received no reply, Keli posted another message six days later: *"Still looking for Andrew Norris – age approx. 38 years ... Has partner Melanie – may now be married."* Again it elicited no response.

Was this just a canny ploy to make it seem as though she was telling the truth about Andrew Norris, or was it a genuine plea for him to come forward? Throughout the entire saga, Keli Lane continually proved herself to be able to keep one step ahead of the authorities. She always had an answer, always had a fresh story; she was never deterred. When one lie was discovered, she seemed to simply invent something new.

Since the gang of 1995 and 1996 had split and gone their separate ways, Keli told police the people she and Andrew had commonly known in those days were no longer her friends. And because she no longer had a mobile phone number for him, she could think of no way of getting in contact with him. In his 2003 interview with Keli Detective Senior Constable Gaut became impatient and frustrated.

"Can you tell me any person who can verify that this Norris exists?" he asked.

"I don't know where to contact any of them," Keli replied. "I haven't spoken [to] or seen these people for six years. The people that are in my life now weren't necessarily around then, they wouldn't have known him."

However Keli had told police that there was one person who could help verify her story – her friend and fellow student from The Australian College of Physical Education, Lisa Andreatta, knew all about Andrew Norris and the baby, she claimed. But Keli said that she had not managed to get in contact with Lisa. And it was during the 2003 interview that Keli also claimed to have emailed friends to try and find out where Lisa was now living, but with no luck.

But this time Detective Senior Constable Gaut was leaps ahead of Keli Lane – way out in front! He broke the news to a shocked Keli that he had managed to locate and make contact with Lisa Andreatta in the United Kingdom. And that what she had told him came as a huge shock – she revealed to him that she had only recently seen her old uni pal Keli Lane, when Keli was holidaying in Europe with her fiancé and child!

Det. Sen. Con. Gaut: "I've been told that you stayed with Lisa Andreatta in England this Christmas."

Ms Lane: "No."

Det. Sen. Con. Gaut: "Or you visited her?"

Ms Lane: "I saw her."

Keli posted an internet message: *"Looking for Andrew Norris ..."* Was it a genuine plea for him to come forward, or was it just a ploy to back up the story she had told the police?

Det. Sen. Con. Gaut: "Did you say that police wanted to speak to her?"

Ms Lane: "No, I did not."

Keli explained that her husband, herself and their daughter had gone to England to visit her in-laws, so they could meet their granddaughter. Lisa had caught the train from London to Suffolk (in England's east) to come and see her at their home. Before Keli left Sydney, she had spoken to Lisa on the phone, but she insisted that she did not have a number for her – it was Lisa who had rung her from a pay phone. During their four-day catch up the police investigation was not mentioned, because Keli said she didn't want Lisa to have to become involved. In her mind if the police could just find Andrew and have him confirm her story, then no one would ever have to know what had happened.

Det. Sen. Con. Gaut: "You didn't think it might be important that she was the one person who could verify the fact that ..."

Ms Lane: "But I know she doesn't know where he is."

Det. Sen. Con. Gaut: "Yeah, but you agree that you said that she knew about the child and she knew who the father was and all that and she could verify that?"

Ms Lane: "Yes."

Lisa Andreatta told the detective via email that she knew nothing about a child being born to Keli Lane in 1996 and that the name

Andrew Norris was not familiar. "I've spoken to Lisa," Detective Senior Constable Gaut told Keli. "And she states that she doesn't know any Andrew Norris and she also doesn't know anything about you having a child in 1996. Keli, it's obvious from what you've been telling me and other people that you're not telling us the truth. Now this matter is not a matter that is going to go away."

Rubbing her head with her hands Keli replied: "I know it's not going to go away, but I don't want to hurt everybody around me."

"We have to know what the truth is," Detective Senior Constable Gaut pressed. "This person Andrew Norris, he's not the father of the child is he?" But Keli stuck to her guns – yes, Andrew Norris was the father and, yes, Tegan was with him. She just didn't have any idea where they might be.

Det. Sen. Con. Gaut: "Why did you say that Lisa Andreatta knows who he is and knew about the child? It's obviously a blatant lie because I've spoken to her."

Ms Lane: "I know she didn't know about the baby, but I am sure she knew who Andrew was, because she used to be there when he was there."

Det. Sen. Con. Gaut: "It doesn't make sense to me, why would you tell me that she knew about the baby and him if you knew that she couldn't support that?"

Ms Lane: "Because I went to uni with her every day and I just ..."

Det. Sen. Con. Gaut: "You thought she might lie for you if she got the opportunity? I can assume that if you're going to nominate a person who you believe knows about the birth of the child it would be a special person because you'd know exactly who knows about the child and who wouldn't. Now I don't believe that was just a mistake. Now it's your opportunity to tell us."

Exasperated once more, the detective explained to Keli that it was a simple inquiry. If the police could establish that this man actually existed and that the child was with him, then it would all go away! Keli could move on with her life, but that wasn't going to happen until police could determine one way or another whether the child was dead or alive. Detective Senior Constable Gaut just couldn't understand all the deception – if the child really was with its natural father, then why not just tell hospital staff the truth from the start?

On May 19, 2003 Keli agreed to accompany Detective Senior Constable Gaut and Detective Sergeant Gavin Beck to the Balmain area to try and find the apartment where she said Andrew Norris had lived with his girlfriend Mel. As it was many years since Keli had socialised in that part of Sydney, she struggled to remember where it was. To help her out the detectives drove to the Town Hall Hotel. From there Keli had said it was a five to 10 minute walk. It was a time-consuming task looking for the unit as the suburb was made up of tiny one-way back streets – a headache even for locals to navigate. For three people relatively unfamiliar with the area, it was an utter nightmare and they found themselves going round in circles, revisiting the same street without meaning to. It took some time, but eventually Keli pointed to a block of units at 24 Wisbeach Street.

From Keli's memory Andrew's apartment had been on the first floor of the building, which meant it was either number 10 or 11. When they entered the foyer Keli exclaimed that the underground car park and the entrance were exactly as she recollected! The entryway doors and staircase were vaguely familiar too ...

Now, hearts beating faster with anticipation, the police officers must have really felt they were getting somewhere. The apartment Andrew had taken her to that night – a night that would ultimately change her life forever – had two bedrooms that led off the lounge room, Keli claimed. "It [the block] just looked familiar," she told police. "But I wouldn't know if the tiles were exactly the same or not."

Keli claimed to have visited the unit about six times over a six-month period and always in the very early hours of the morning. She would often head straight to water-polo training after her visits – which was a short walk away at The Dawn Fraser Pool in Balmain. "How was it that you stayed over if he was living there with a girlfriend?" Detective Senior Constable Gaut asked. "He'd just offer, I mean there wasn't an arrangement." The times Keli did sleep over, she said Mel obviously wasn't there. From what she knew Mel worked in retail and she wasn't married to Andrew.

In the months before taking Keli to Balmain to re-trace her steps to Andrew's unit, Keli said she had searched for the apartment herself for about half-an-hour one afternoon with no luck. "Do you agree that it's highly unlikely that this might be the unit that you had in mind?" asked Detective Senior Constable Gaut at their next interview in January 2004. His comment surprised Keli as she felt she had described it so well. "I think it's more likely that it's the right one," she replied.

Detective Senior Constable Gaut had his reasons for asking. After Keli had pinpointed 24 Wisbeach Street, he had put in a call to the local real estate agent to check their records and once again Keli's story didn't add up.

Real estate agent Mathew John Klein was not working in the area in 1995/96, however his employer Ray White Real Estate had been responsible for leasing out all the units at 24 Wisbeach Street. Checking back through documentation, it didn't take Mr Klein long to realise that there was no one by the name of Andrew Norris on their files. In fact, at the time Keli claimed to have been sleeping over at the unit, it was being rented by a Mr Shaun Greaves.

Shaun Greaves was 37 years old by the time police spoke to him in July 2003 – the same age Keli said Andrew Norris would have been – but he didn't match the profile Keli had provided. He said he had always lived alone, but that he had never met or seen Keli Lane before. Real estate agent Mr Klein backed up the claim that Mr Greaves did not have housemates. Anyone else staying at the unit would have had to fill in an application form and show proof of identity, so the agent would have known.

"What about if a person comes in and lists two or three other people, do you check their identification?" Sergeant Becroft asked him at the inquest. "We ask that they do fill out an application form with all their details, and [attach] a copy of their licence," he explained. "Whether they go on the lease or not is irrelevant as long as we know who is in the property."

Mr Klein said it was possible that someone else had moved in without the agent knowing about it, but since inspections were done every three to four months, it was unlikely that the real estate office wouldn't have found out. Mr Klein was surprised that Keli had said the block looked the same as when she had visited back in 1996, because in the meantime it had been sold and in 2003 all of the apartments were renovated. Now Detective Senior Constable Gaut was almost satisfied that Mr Greaves was not the man they were looking for. However, wanting to be thorough, he refused to let the matter rest and went in search of Greaves's former neighbours.

Brothers Peter and Steven Clark lived at number 11 around the time Keli said she paid a visit to the unit across the hall. "You've never seen her before?" Sergeant Becroft asked Peter at the inquest. "Only in the newspapers," replied Peter, who now recognised Keli Lane from her face being flashed across TV screens and newspaper front pages.

Peter admitted that he had very little to do with other residents in the building. "I don't know anyone by name," he explained. "I could only tell him by the face. Me and my brother are both very private people and we don't really make a point of … even with my wife at the unit I'm at now, I couldn't tell you many of the people's full names. At the time I was there the first guy I remember was a bit of a chubby guy. After that I think it was a Sri Lankan family, and then a French family."

The brothers lived in the unit from August 1995 until March 2003. When they were shown a picture of Shaun Greaves, Peter confirmed that it was the guy who lived across the hall. He was absolutely certain that he had lived alone and Steven agreed with him. "Do you recall whether he had any other people perhaps staying with him during that period of late-'95, mid-'96?" he was asked. "No, he very much kept to himself. The only time you'd see him was when he'd open the door and he'd get pizzas delivered all the time. It's the only time I ever saw him, and I never ever spoke to him."

What was also puzzling police was that in early 1996, a man by the name of Tom Lane had given his address as Unit 10, 24 Wisbeach Street when he was arrested on a minor matter. To Detective Senior Constable Gaut it seemed too much of a coincidence that a man with the same last name as Keli had claimed to have lived in that apartment at such a crucial time. "You don't know any Tom Lane?" Detective Senior Constable Gaut had asked Keli. "No," she replied. "Okay, and you're not aware of having a relative by the name of Tom Lane?" – "No, we have a very small family, I would know." Keli's parents also denied knowing any person by that name. Another red herring.

Keli told police she had tried to search for a mobile phone number for Andrew, but stressed that during the brief time she was sleeping with him she hadn't been allowed to ring it. "He made it pretty clear," she said, "not to contact him in case someone else answered the phone." From what she could recall she had only ever called him twice and one of those occasions was to tell him that she had checked herself into Auburn Hospital to have the baby. "Can you explain to me," said Detective Senior Constable Gaut. "If Andrew Norris was the natural father, why you didn't just give Andrew Norris' name on the (hospital records) as the contact person? If he was the person who you say you contacted to come to the hospital, you were expecting him to come to the hospital, why didn't you just put his name down?" He waited patiently as Keli thought about her answer. "'Cause he didn't want any record of that," she eventually replied. "He didn't want me, he did not want anything to do with me."

What Detective Senior Constable Gaut couldn't get through to Keli was that if she had told hospital staff that Andrew Norris was the father in the first place, as opposed to claiming it was Duncan Gillies, then there would be a permanent record – a consistent and unconflicting one – at the hospital, and the police wouldn't be so suspicious of her story.

In her 2001 interview with police, Keli had said that she had Andrew's number in a box of old papers that she thought she may have left in the garage of Duncan's Gladesville house when they broke up in March 1998. "I've lived in three different places (since then)," she explained, "and I've thrown out a hell of a lot of stuff, and I've lost a lot of stuff because when Duncan and I broke up, it was pretty much on the day and I didn't get a lot of my things back."

She said she had followed up on her promise to try and find the number some time in October 2002, but when she dropped in at the Gladesville house, the new tenants weren't helpful. "There were people there renting," she told Detective Senior Constable Gaut. "And they wouldn't let me, they just said no. They said there was nothing in there that had been left."

What Keli didn't know was that the three women living in the house at that time were police officers! And officers Leah Horden, Sharon Smithers and Tracey Grey, were easily able to state for the record that no one had ever come to their door asking to search through boxes in the garage. "Well, I know I did," Keli insisted, "because I went there on my way to work and I knocked on the door and I asked, would there be anything left in the garage."

"These are all policewomen," said Detective Senior Constable Gaut, incredulous that Keli was still sticking to her tale. "Keli, like I said before, this matter isn't going to go away, it's a matter that the child is missing. It's a suspected death. Our investigations show that you're not telling us the truth, we can't track the child's existence, we can't track the alleged father of the child, none of your family knows about the birth of the child."

Fearing the investigation was going absolutely nowhere in early November 2004, Detective Senior Constable Gaut wrote to the Missing Persons Unit in Parramatta asking for their help in finding Andrew Norris. It was Senior Constable Darren Conabeer who lent a hand, but he too had little success. "I had no result on the month and year supplied," he said referring to the birth checks that he had conducted on Andrew Norris.

Senior Constable Conabeer explained that he personally was involved in investigating anywhere between three and 10 missing person cases a week, and at any one time could have as many as 150 on his books. In NSW an average of 9000 people are reported missing each year. In 99 per cent of those cases, the missing person turns up or is located within a two-month time frame. As of June 2005, he said there were 650 missing person cases being investigated in NSW, where the missing person in question hadn't been heard from or seen in more than 12 months. Tegan Lane fell into that category. "I'd say NSW is the forerunner in terms of missing persons cases," he boasted. "We dedicate the resources and the money to making sure that missing person cases are solved to the best of our ability."

But the tragedy of Tegan Lee Lane's case was that so much time had elapsed since she had "disappeared", and in the short time since police had been trying to trace her, they had been frustrated and critically misled by a mass of inaccurate information.

Coroner Abernethy was frustrated, though, by the inability of police to track down Mr Norris. "One of the problems in this case," he stated wearily, "is that we're relying on estimates about the age of this Andrew Norris. We're not really sure if that's the name, [we] think it is, that's what we've been told [but] that age may be wrong." Mr Abernethy seriously doubted that the father's name was Norris and asked about a possible search being conducted for someone by the name of Morris, the other surname Keli had given Andrew earlier on. However Senior Constable Conabeer said that extending the search with such a name as popular as "Morris" over the six to seven year time frame, would return thousands of possibilities.

It was the mix-up with the so-called father Andrew's last name that Keli's lawyer Peter Hamill pounced on when Detective Senior Constable Gaut gave evidence at the inquest. He believed that was the fault of police – that they failed to hear what Keli had said correctly during an interview – and not that Keli had changed her story.

The interview was re-played to the court and we all listened to it. However, Keli does not actually say the name on tape – she had given it to Detective Senior Constable Kehoe before the formal recorded interview. Only Kehoe says the name on the tape – which is clearly Morris. The point is that Keli didn't correct him, although to be fair they are similar sounding names. What Keli's lawyer Peter Hamill later criticises is that police made no effort to ask her to spell out the name. This is what we heard played back in court:

Det. Sen. Con. Kehoe: "You told me that the person that you, that is the natural father of the child, is Andrew Morris. Is that correct?
Ms Lane: "That's correct.")

Mr Hamill also felt that Detective Senior Constable Gaut had made up his mind about what had happened on September 14, 1996 – the day Keli Lane and baby Tegan left Auburn Hospital – before he had even spoken to Keli.

"By the time you became involved you were suspicious of her, were you not?" he asked.

"Actually, I wasn't when I first spoke to her," answered Detective Senior Constable Gaut. "I was simply seeing if there was anything in the story she had given [that would provide] further information to locate Andrew Norris. That was the reason for bringing her in, that was the reason for not making an electronically recorded interview because at that stage I was thinking stranger things have happened, I was looking into what she had told us."

But Mr Hamill was of the firm belief that the mix-up with the surname Morris or Norris was the fault of police and not Keli. And it was the critical confusion over the surname that had held up the investigation.

Mr Hamill: "A major discrepancy as you saw it was the difference between the surname Morris and the surname Norris?"

Det. Sen. Con. Gaut: "Well, that meant I had to start making inquiries into Norris as opposed to Morris."

Mr Hamill: "Is the answer to that a simple yes? Was it an important discrepancy as far as you were concerned?"

Det. Sen. Con. Gaut: "Yeah, it was a very important discrepancy."

Mr Hamill: "The Norris and the Morris?"

Det. Sen. Con. Gaut: "Yes, it was."

It was Mr Hamill's belief then that Keli had always said Andrew's surname was Norris, right from the very start. In fact it was police officer Detective Senior Constable Kehoe who had misheard her during their interview, not Keli who had changed her story, Keli's lawyer claimed. He accused the police of not taking the proper precautions in the 2001 interview to clarify the spelling of the last name.

Regardless, police didn't believe that Andrew Norris or Morris was the father's name. However, Keli's husband said that he did, despite all the failed attempts to find Andrew Norris. "From what Keli's told me," he said at the inquest, "she's 100 per cent sure that that's the person's name. So again I wasn't there at the time so I can't say anything other than that."

"Do you believe it's possible that Keli gave the child to someone other than an Andrew Norris, in your opinion?" Sergeant Becroft asked him. "No," he replied.

Keli Lane's husband was unwavering in his support of his wife's claim that "missing" Tegan's father did exist. But then to have been anything else would have meant considering the chilling alternatives.

Was eight-year-old Tegan living happily with her dad Andrew Norris somewhere in Australia? It was a nice thought, but looking increasingly doubtful.

the search for tegan

A NEAR MISS AND A DEAD END

HOW DO YOU start looking for a child who has not been seen or heard of since she was two days old? Police were already hampered in their search for a number of reasons. No one at Auburn Hospital had actually witnessed Keli Lane leave the hospital on September 14, 1996, let alone knew where she and baby Tegan were headed. Midwife Ann Marie Hanlon did remember Keli's request to be discharged from hospital just two days after the birth, but when she wrote her discharge report at 2pm, she confirmed to police: "The room was empty, the bed was empty, the cot was empty and all her [Keli's] personal belongings had gone."

Keli Lane claimed she had handed over baby Tegan to her natural father, Andrew Norris, in the hospital car park and then driven home. But an extensive search to find the elusive Mr Norris had proved fruitless. He was a mystery man whose very existence was increasingly coming into question. On top of that, Keli had discharged herself from hospital before the all-important Guthrie Spot test had been taken – which would have provided police with Tegan's DNA – so it was impossible to determine for sure who really was the baby's father.

It was hard not to imagine if, as everyone hoped and prayed, Tegan Lane were still alive what she would look like now at eight years old. Would she take after the mother who had bundled her into her arms and discharged herself from Auburn Hospital on that unusually warm September day in 1996? Would she have blond hair and be growing into an athletic frame? Would she be smart, sporty, a member of her school netball team, or, a strong swimmer, showing signs of following her birth mother's love of water-polo? Most of all, would she be happy and safe?

Did she have any inkling of the circumstances of her birth and who her mother was? Might she have glanced up at the television one night and heard a news reporter talk about missing baby Tegan? Had she sensed attempts by her protective adoptive mum and dad to hide newspaper stories about the case that had gripped Australia?

Amid all this speculation one thing was certain – all attempts, both in Australia and overseas, to determine who Tegan's father was had now failed. So how on earth were police ever going to track down a little girl who had simply vanished into thin air?

The tough job for Detective Senior Constable Gaut was that he had to prove a negative – that Tegan Lane was *not* dead.

His starting point was Michael Coghlan from the NSW Department of Births, Deaths and Marriages. Mr Coghlan had been working for the department for five years when Detective Senior Constable Gaut approached him with a mammoth task – he desperately needed help in tracking down a little girl born on September 12, 1996. Initially it seemed like a pretty straightforward request, until Mr Coghlan was informed of the mega twist: there was the very real possibility that the child's parents had registered her birth under a different date and/or name, that is if she was registered at all!

Mr Coghlan initially decided to keep the search simple, so began – optimistically – by entering the exact name and birth date as given to him by Detective Senior Constable Gaut into the database. If only it could have been that easy! He very quickly found out that there was no child registered as Tegan Lane, who was born on 12/9/96.

Initially it seemed easy enough – to track down a record of a girl born on September 12, 1996. The problem was that the child's parents might not have registered her at all.

It cemented in Mr Coghlan's mind an existing lack of confidence in the system by which babies were registered in New South Wales. It was the parents' sole responsibility to register their newborn and if they failed to do so, the maximum penalty for not complying was just $1,100. Plus, there was no uniform legislation in Australia – instead each state and territory had its own system for registering births and it was not strictly policed. From Mr Coghlan's memory no one had ever been fined for *not* registering their child. "Over the last few years," explained Coghlan at the 2005 inquest, "each of the eight jurisdictions in Australia has moved to create a model legislation where there are similar provisions under each of our forms – to try and have a more consistent approach."

Facing the impossible task of helping Detective Senior Constable Gaut trace Tegan Lane, Mr Coghlan was more sure than ever that a stricter country-wide policy for registering births in Australia was well overdue. But it didn't help him now, in the short term, to try and find Tegan. In this case he knew that a much more drastic – and time consuming – method would be needed if he was to locate the missing child. He gathered his staff together and gave them a period of possible birth dates to search. They were to cross-check every birth record between March 31, 1996 and September 30, 1997 against any midwifery or hospital records. This was not a task that could be knocked over in a couple of weeks – according to the database the number of children born between those dates was 86,430!

Firstly Mr Coghlan wrote to the NSW Department of Health, requesting a list of all hospital notifications with regard to births and a list of Midwife Collection sheets. Whenever a child is born in NSW not only does the hospital notify the Department of Health, a midwife will also fill out what is known as a "Midwife Data Collection sheet", which can be used to cross-check births against hospital records if needed. If a child is born at home, the midwife has a legal responsibility to notify the authorities, although the actual registration of the birth can only be done by a parent, not a midwife or hospital.

(The case of "missing baby Tegan Lane" led to the NSW Government introducing new laws in June 2007. They rule that midwives must alert authorities of a baby's birth within seven days. New South Wales hospitals – which previously had three weeks to notify the Department of Births, Deaths and Marriages of a birth – will also only have a week to register the birth.)

Mr Coghlan was surprised when he received a relatively prompt reply from the NSW Health Department. He took their details and compared them against his own department's database. Of the more than 86,000 births shown on his database, the health department computer crossmatched the data and identified 1,200 entries with which there was some sort of discrepancy. That is, certain information which needed to be clarified or which did not match the corresponding hospital records. That was when the real work began.

The 1,200 birth records were divided among his staff each of whom began a manual search – faxing and phoning the relevant hospitals, until the fresh information they gleaned narrowed the number of questionable records down to 729.

Again Mr Coghlan was concerned that there were more than 700 registered births in NSW that needed to be investigated, due to fraudulent entries or simply incorrect information – whether that was accidental or intentional. This was unquestionably an alarming trend to have uncovered.

It took many long months of exhaustive inquiries, but finally Mr Coghlan handed a list of eight names to Detective Senior Constable Gaut – not a list of persons who he believed could be Tegan Lane, but rather the children that his staff simply could not locate or identify. The biggest problem Mr Coghlan and his staff had faced was that a number of the families had moved in the eight years since Tegan was born. Those who had relocated several times – especially if they had shifted interstate or overseas – were impossible to track.

Even so, to have just eight unexplained births from an initial list of more than 86,000 was a laudable result. Every other birth from that time period had been accounted for, double checked and confirmed. "With the exception of those eight," said Mr Coghlan, "my opinion would be that on the basis of conducting such a thorough search, we can say that from the information reliant on hospital notifications and the notifications received by other parents, that it appears that none of those would match Tegan Lane."

But the system he had relied upon was far from accurate. It depended on the diligence of the Health Department in gathering the Midwife Data Collection sheets and the hospital records of each birth.

"If any of those records had been provided fraudulently or were inaccurate," he explained, "then there is the possibility Tegan Lane is registered under another name." He said that while it is an offence to do so, there is little to no chance of parents being caught, as cross-checks are never done!

Indeed the system for registering births was far from ideal and, as Keli's lawyer Mr Hamill pointed out to Detective Senior Constable Gaut, the research carried out by Mr Coghlan and his staff could well be rife with errors.

Mr Hamill: "It can't be ruled out that her birth was registered but registered in a different name with a different birth date or a different hospital?"

Det. Sen. Con. Gaut: "Illegally?

Mr Hamill: "Well, yeah, illegally."

Det. Sen. Con. Gaut: "Illegally, well, I don't know."

Mr Hamill: "You can't rule out the possibility that Ms Lane gave this child to the father who registered it perhaps illegally under another name?"

Det. Sen. Con. Gaut: "I can't rule out any possibility."

There was also a real concern that Tegan's birth had been registered interstate and not in New South Wales, although that would have been hard to do. When a hospital hands parents a registration form after the child is born, it has already been marked with that particular hospital's stamp. "We have quite distinct birth registration forms provided by hospitals," said Mr Coghlan "so that if a state was to be in receipt of another state's form it would raise immediate concern. I believe other states have similar processes that we do, where the forms are pre-stamped by hospitals and only provided by hospitals on a one-off basis to parents."

Mr Hamill was not convinced, though, that those types of measures were enough to prevent mistakes. "We can't rule out the possibility of a falsely registered birth in that period?" he questioned. "With the exception of the work we've done to match them to the best of our endeavours," answered Mr Coghlan. "Beyond that my only opinion would be to say that if the original information given to the hospital or midwives was fraudulent, if so then obviously that's a separate issue."

Poring through Auburn Hospital's birth records from September 1996 Detective Senior Constable Gaut noticed the other baby girl delivered on the same day as Tegan, who sadly was stillborn. That child's birth had been registered, but it crossed Detective Senior Constable Gaut's mind that perhaps Keli had met this woman in hospital and they had talked. He could not rule out the possibility that the pair had organised some kind of deal, where the bereaved mother of the stillborn would take custody of Tegan. It was a stab in the dark, but worth looking at.

As it happened – happily for the mum of the stillborn – she had since given birth to two other children, neither of whom could possibly have been Tegan. The woman also confirmed to Detective Senior Constable Gaut that she had never met Keli Lane during her time in Auburn Hospital.

It was a line of questioning worth following up, but Detective Senior Constable Gaut was way off track and now he was right back where he started, with no clue as to where Tegan might be.

But even if the mystery of Tegan Lane is never solved, her disappearance will always be pivotal in saving other babies who may have got lost in the nebulous system for registering births in Australia. As a result of the Tegan case, the NSW Department of Births, Deaths and Marriages has instituted major changes in the way in which births are registered and moved to tighten any loopholes, the most recent being new laws ensuring midwives and hospitals notify authorities of any births within a seven-day period.

Mr Coghlan said he is now trying to identify any backlog of births not registered within the prescribed 60-day period, going back as far as 1993. "The onus has always been clearly on the parent to register the event within that time frame," he said but admitted the system had been too relaxed. He said Tegan's case highlighted the desperate need for change and that as of February 2006, the Department had issued 8,700 letters to parents reminding them that they had yet to register their child's birth.

He had received a large number of replies to those letters. "The Registry has taken its role quite seriously in bringing to the attention of parents their responsibility of registering the birth," he said.

Under today's new procedure – which came into being in July 2005 – a letter is sent at 80 days to inform parents of their legal obligation to return the registration form. If the form is not received, a second letter is sent at six months. An additional 1,800 births have been placed on the database since the new policy has been implemented. Mr Coghlan explained that his staff send out anywhere between 500 and 700 letters a week.

Coroner Abernethy: "Are you confident now that the checks and balances you have implemented in the last year or two are sufficient?"

Mr Coghlan: "We still have an issue where we are reliant on the CEOs of hospitals and midwives to notify us within 21 days as required under our legislation, unfortunately we only have coverage of about 89 per cent of those events. It appears that a lot of those notifications are not being received from private hospitals."

Since then talks have commenced with the Australian Private Hospitals Association to work together with the Department to ensure every child is registered.

For Tegan, though, the changes have come too late. Coroner John Abernethy suggested that the very least that could be done was for Tegan's birth to still be registered, to make her status legal. But Keli

Even if Tegan Lane was registered under a different first name and different surname, one fact remains: there was no child who was registered on that date at that hospital.

Lane, still insistent that Tegan was with her natural father, said she was shocked that her daughter's birth had not been registered by the father. "I don't understand why he wouldn't have done that," she told police.

"There's never been any person [registered]," Detective Senior Constable Gaut explained to her. "Even if Tegan was registered under a different first name, different surname, no child has been registered with Births, Deaths and Marriages in NSW for that date at that hospital." Keli was stunned. "So all the paperwork that the hospital gave me that then got passed onto him, my part's gone through and his part hasn't?" she queried. "I don't know what part you took," Detective Senior Constable Gaut replied.

Keli claimed that the agreement she'd had with Tegan's father – the mysterious Andrew Norris police had been unable to trace – was that she would take care of all the medical forms such as Medicare, and he would register the birth. "I've made enquiries with Medicare," said Detective Senior Constable Gaut, "and it shows Tegan Lane was enrolled on your card, but [with the wrong birth date] on September 19, 1996, and it also shows that Tegan Lane has had no medical services for which a Medicare benefit has been claimed." Detective Senior Constable Gaut had checked with both Medicare and the Health Insurance Commission – no transactions had ever gone through under the name Tegan Lane.

A jumpy Keli claimed the reason for that was because her daughter Tegan had never been in her care. "But do you agree," asked Detective Senior Constable Gaut, "it would be very odd for a child of that age, or up to the age of six or seven not to need any medical help? It shows that the child hasn't been in existence for quite a few years. There is no record with Tegan being enrolled as a student with any New South Wales public or central school, Catholic or private schools."

In March 2005 Detective Senior Constable Gaut made a request to the education department of each state and territory to send out forms asking school staff to double check the background of any child remotely matching Tegan's birth date, name or any link to a man by the name of Andrew Norris. It was a huge ask from the very start: time consuming for the already busy schools and not exactly high on their list of priorities. When Detective Senior Constable Gaut took the stand in the final days of the inquest in February 2006, he came armed with six volumes of material from schools from around the country.

He explained that when he had made his initial request it had been met with a lacklustre response – a number of schools hadn't replied – but as the case gathered momentum and received more publicity, and after some particularly harsh criticism from the Coroner, shamed schools started to oblige and make an effort to help find missing Tegan. That's when the forms started flowing in.

The search for Tegan Lee Lane was always going to be a daunting one for Detective Senior Constable Gaut. His hands were well and truly tied, with a lack of information, a lapful of misinformation and a lack of co-operation from the one person you would expect to want to help in finding her missing baby – the mother herself! To a member of the public, not having taken an oath to serve the community, it would almost be tempting to say, why bother?

Even so, Detective Senior Constable Gaut was attacked by Keli Lane's lawyer, Mr Hamill, for the delay in approaching the schools, which did not begin in earnest until March 2005. Detective Senior Constable Gaut explained the obvious deficiencies in such a search – the most arduous being getting all of the schools to respond. Initially his team started with New South Wales, hoping that state-wide would be a wide enough search. In the end they realised – as they had countless times before in this investigation – if the job was to be done properly, the search would have to be expanded. And in widening the search came inaccuracies in the replies. "Those searches [for NSW] came back," he explained. "The schools [authorities] did the searches, sent out memos to all the schools, whether they be Catholic, Independent or Public. When they did the search they didn't get replies from all the memos. Instead they took the non-replies as meaning that schools under them had searched their records and had nothing so they did not reply. Now, when it was recently suggested that we go through those NSW schools again, this time we asked them to get replies in writing from all the schools. Now it was at that stage I suggested that if we're going to do NSW we may as well do the whole of Australia."

"You agree that any such searches with schools involve a very high possibility of human error?" asked Mr Hamill. "That's correct," Detective Senior Constable Gaut replied before the Coroner interjected. "Or human lack of diligence just doing the check." Coroner Abernethy agreed that there were many opportunities for the search to go wrong, but accepted that there was simply no other alternative if a school-based search was to be done.

As the school search continued, it became more and more problematic. Each state and territory devised its own questionnaire, so there was a lack of consistency in questioning and time after time forms came back with errors.

"Each state I asked basically to look for that date of birth, Andrew Norris, or if there is no father listed, to give us that information and we can follow up and make sure there's no link," explained Detective Senior Constable Gaut.

In Western Australia – for example, a form was sent out which read as follows:

Please Tick the Boxes:
❐ *A search has been made*
❐ *A search has produced no results*

....

[a third line was left here for the school to add any extra relevant information they felt may be helpful to the police]

"In the process of that simple form filling out exercise, something like 20 or 30 of the responses didn't tick the box that said you've made a record check," said Mr Hamill. "What I am saying to you is that there are many opportunities for the search to go wrong and break down as a result of human error."

No one disagreed, but what was the alternative? Mr Hamill didn't have one.

But then suddenly Detective Senior Constable Gaut hit the jackpot! Four months after he had put out the plea to Australia's schools, he received the call he had been waiting for.

It was the morning of June 9, 2005. A school more than 1000 kilometres away from Sydney in a town called Eagleby – between Brisbane and the Gold Coast in Queensland – reported that they had a student who could possibly be Tegan! Her details were eerily similar to the missing child's – her name was Teagan Chapman (her Christian name spelt with an extra "a"), she was born on September 12, 1996 and she had a connection to a man by the name of Norris; a man called Allen Norris was listed on her birth certificate as her father.

It wasn't the first time the detective's hopes had been raised during the investigation into missing Tegan Lane. Previously it had seemed he may have found the unit in Balmain where her natural father Andrew Norris was supposed to have lived, only to have his hopes dashed.

Was he on a winning streak this time around? Could this really be the missing piece of the jigsaw, the end of the investigation he took on in October 2002?

Detective Senior Constable Gaut immediately called the Coroner's assisting counsel Rebbecca Becroft – in charge of the day-to-day running of the inquest – and the pair wasted no time in jumping on a flight to Queensland to investigate. What was on their minds on their trip north? Had they really found the missing child?

More importantly, had Keli Lane been telling the truth all along and was Tegan with her father?

And what would they do if it was Tegan? It was a sensitive case to handle. But this was the big breakthrough Detective Senior Constable Gaut and Sergeant Becroft had been battling to reach. They both had put their lives on hold – allowed the investigation and the inquest to consume their thoughts on a daily basis – and as a consequence the lives of their families had been affected too. Wouldn't it be nice to put it all behind them – an investigation ending on the best possible note, with a missing child being found safe and well?

Excited – but experienced enough to know not to get their hopes up too much – they disembarked in Queensland; Tegan's files containing the little information they had about her, tucked under their arms.

It was a nail-biting 10 days or so. Sergeant Becroft and Detective Senior Constable Gaut had organised to speak to the child's grandparents while they waited for her medical records to arrive from Mater Children's Hospital in Brisbane. It was also agreed that Teagan Chapman would submit to a DNA test.

And so they all waited anxiously for the results. The call from the hospital came through nine days later on June 18. They were crushed by the results: Teagan Chapman's DNA did not match Keli Lane's; rather it was a match for her mother Debbie Chapman.

In June 2005 Debbie Chapman, 30, gave an interview to *The Australian* newspaper, clearly unhappy that her eight-year-old daughter had been innocently thrust into the limelight. Since the media coverage, complete strangers had told her they doubted the child was her daughter." That really hurts," she told the newspaper. "This is all crap, she's my kid." Meanwhile her daughter Teagan told the newspaper: "I'm Teagan Shanice Chapman and I hope they find Tegan Lane soon."

It seemed all Teagan Chapman from Queensland had in common with the missing baby born in Sydney, was her Christian name and the day she was born – plus an uncanny similarity of the name of the man listed as her father (it would turn out that Allen Norris was present at Teagan Chapman's birth but was not her biological father), with that of Tegan Lane's supposedly natural father. But that would be where the similarity would end. On the one hand bitterly disappointed that this child wasn't the Tegan they were looking for, and that they were still no closer to solving the mystery, the officers equally must have felt relief that this little girl's parentage was not in question and that she could go living her life as normal.

When he touched down back in Sydney after his abortive mission to Queensland, the next stage of Detective Senior Constable Gaut's

With no signs that Tegan Lee Lane was alive, the police began the grim task of collecting records from the morgue. Was there any evidence of an unidentified baby's body?

search was to be a macabre one. With no signs that Tegan Lee Lane was alive, he began the grim task of collecting records from the morgue to ascertain whether they were in possession of any evidence of either an unidentified newborn baby's body, or body parts. He put officer Carolyn Ebstein in charge of those inquiries, but her trip to Glebe Morgue in Sydney's inner west did not uncover any new information. She pored through the list of unidentified skeletons, body parts and bones, but nothing was a match for baby Tegan.

Finally, on June 23, 2005, Coroner John Abernethy made his own plea for the Australian public to come forward with information. "I'd simply make the appeal that at this stage of this inquest, if there is a couple out there, be they from NSW or elsewhere in Australia, who has this child without the child being legally adopted, this is their opportunity to come forward and give that information to either an adoption agency or preferably the officer-in-charge of this case."

To encourage public assistance, there was a reminder of the assurance Centacare's Angharad Candlin had given the inquest when she was asked by Sergeant Becroft about the possibility of the child's current parents being allowed to keep Tegan if they came forward.

Sgt. Becroft: "If Tegan Lane is still alive and whoever the parents of that child [happen to be] would come forward today, would they be able to go through the adoption process and legally adopt Tegan Lane?"

Ms Candlin: "Yes. If Keli signed a consent for her adoption, absolutely yes. In fact, I'd actually think that's probably a good thing to happen, it gives her permanence and it gives her legal status."

Sgt. Becroft: "And it would be the case that if that was to happen that Tegan Lane and whoever was raising her came forward that all of those inquiries would be dealt with very discreetly and that none of their details be made public to anyone?"

Ms Candlin: "No."

Sgt. Becroft: "So privacy would be ensured?"

Ms Candlin: "Yes [that is] absolutely paramount to adoption."

Ms Candlin pointed out that under adoption laws it is illegal to identify either party involved in an adoption. In fact, even allowing Keli Lane's details to be released and made public, was technically a breach of the Adoption Act. Coroner Abernethy had only lifted that suppression on identifying Keli Lane in the hope someone would come forward with vital information.

Protecting the identity of the two other children Keli had legally adopted – the girl born in 1995 and the son born in 1999 – was of premium concern to Ms Candlin too.

She revealed that both sets of adoptive parents of the girl and the boy respectively, were fearful at this time that too much information had already been released, and that their adoptive offspring could be identified. On hearing Ms Candlin's concerns, Coroner Abernethy reiterated the need for the media to tread cautiously.

(We – the court reporters – were always well aware and respectful of our legal responsibilities while reporting this coronial inquest. While the media knew it was free to report on Keli Lane, no one had ever mentioned her other two children by name; their identities were protected.)

"I've warned the media over and over again," said Coroner Abernethy "to keep off the subject. Mention the fact of two children, but leave it at that and if it is more than that – and I share your concern [Ms Candlin] – I simply reiterate again for the media to be very, very careful. A little girl and a little boy now have very different lives and if [they are] ever connected as being part of this that would be most unfortunate for their upbringing and their livelihood, their well-being in life. It's such a serious matter and the media bears an extremely heavy onus to be very careful in how they report this case."

Certainly the press bench came under fire from Keli Lane's family, who said they believed it was the publicity from the case that had stopped Tegan's father from coming forward and presenting himself to police. Keli's younger brother Morgan Lane was openly scornful of the media – he seemed to believe that it was the media's fault that the case had become so widely known, although he also pointed the finger at police. "I can completely understand the motives behind anyone not coming forward," he said, "and the way that episode with how the police and the media handled that child [Teagan] being publicised, it's even greater incentive for someone not to come forward."

Throughout the inquest – often painful because of the intimate line of questioning and reliving of traumatic times – each and every one of Keli's family and friends who took the stand, stood by her. Asked what they thought may have happened to Tegan, they all said unanimously that they believed she was living with her father and, yes, of course she was still alive. They were strong in their views in spite of the fact that Keli had not whispered a word to any of them about what really happened. Perhaps they too had been frightened to ask?

But if anyone was to be believed perhaps it should be her husband, Keli Lane's current partner – who cannot be identified – and father of her fourth child, a girl too, who was emphatic that his wife did not kill Tegan.

Sgt. Becroft: "In your own personal opinion do you think that Keli has done anything to harm Tegan Lane after she left Auburn Hospital?"
Husband: "No, never."
Sgt. Becroft: "What do you base that on?"
Husband: "Well, from our relationship together. She's been a fantastic

wife, a wonderful mother, you know and I love her dearly. There's really no way in the world that she could ever do anything to harm a child."

Keli's immediate family – her parents and brother – were as certain as her husband that she did nothing wrong, but how could they all be so sure? None of them had actually questioned her outright, believing there was no point and not wanting to upset her further. Was there something in the back of their minds preventing them from forcing Keli to open up? Were they just afraid of the truth? "Keli is a beautiful, loving girl," said her mother Sandra. "There's no way she could harm a living soul, especially her own child."

Regardless, the latest round of investigations had resulted in one really positive breakthrough as a result of Tegan Lane's tortuous case. The system for registering births had been tightened up considerably, making it less likely that courts would ever be faced with as tragic a situation as missing Tegan Lane's again. At least her birth hadn't been in vain.

keli takes the stand

WILL THE TRUTH COME OUT?

THE BIGGEST day of the inquest came in late June 2005, when it was finally Keli Lane's turn to take the stand at the coronial inquest into the disappearance of her second baby, Tegan Lee Lane, born on September 12, 1996. By that stage the Coroner had heard from her family and her close friends, from police who had interviewed her and from hospital staff who had cared for her, following three other pregnancies. Yet he was still no closer to determining what had happened to Tegan – he knew the answers rested with Keli, her mother.

It was the morning everyone who had become intrigued by the investigation – the press, the public too – had been waiting for. It was probably the morning Keli Lane had been dreading since the police investigation was launched four years before.

As she had every morning, Keli arrived at the court shortly before 9am on June 27, accompanied by her father Robert Lane. She was dressed in what had become her trademark outfit: a dark blue/black suit and a collared shirt, which on this occasion happened to be bright pink. Perhaps she thought the colour would give her a boost on a day she knew was going to be tough.

As Keli made the 30-metre walk from her car to the courthouse, the newspaper photographers started frantically snapping away, elbowing and jostling for the best vantage point. Television cameramen too struggled to film Keli's arrival; retreating backwards at a hurried pace, cameras balanced on their shoulders, trying to get a steady full face-on "Keli Lane arrival shot". It was a shot that would be flashed across screens in that night's evening news bulletins, a shot that would attempt to capture Keli's inner turmoil.

There was indeed an intense buzz among the media pack that morning. A close-knit group, we court reporters would usually wait outside the courtroom each morning, drinking coffee, chatting and reading the newspapers. Until, bang on 10am, when we'd make a rush for the press bench, to take the first of many shorthand notes that day, scribbling verbatim what the Coroner, police officers and witnesses had to say.

But this day was different. There was less time for convivial chat between the reporters – everyone was anxious to secure their seat in the tiny courtroom, and had started moving in as soon as Keli had entered the building. There was one thing on all of our minds – were we finally about to hear the truth?

Unusually the very punctual Coroner, John Abernethy, was running late, which added to the drama of the occasion. By the time he had settled on the bench at 10:20am – instead of the usual prompt 10am start – it was standing room only in court. Glancing briefly in Keli's direction, he took a deep breath and said in a loud voice that he didn't want to hear from her that morning! There was an audible gasp from all those present – including Keli who looked up from her lap, where her head had been hung low – why wouldn't he want to hear from the person at the centre of the mystery?

But Coroner Abernethy had his reasons: he had spent a restless night trying to work out how he should approach Keli's evidence. In the end he had decided that he didn't want to hear from her, well at least not yet! He wanted to adjourn the case to allow police more time to search for Tegan, and more time to forensically examine the car Keli was driving in 1996 (in which she claimed to have driven away from the hospital, after handing Tegan to her natural father, the elusive Andrew Norris).

He also told Keli Lane's lawyer, Peter Hamill, that his client should look at undergoing a psychiatric assessment: "It wouldn't be a bad idea," he said, "for your client to see a psychiatrist and see if we can get a report on her behalf. That's entirely up to her, I can't force her."

Abernethy was hoping a psychiatric assessment of Keli would provide valuable insight into a disappearance he described as "surreal" and "bizarre".

"If in fact the child is alive," he said, he wanted anyone who knew a couple "hitherto childless, who all of a sudden had a child" to come forward to police. It was the second plea he had made to the Australian public to come forward and help in this baffling inquiry.

Coroner Abernethy also ordered that all of the transcripts of interviews with Keli, and the police brief of evidence, be sent to a forensic psychiatrist for evaluation. He had a message too for any school in the country that was yet to return the questionnaire Detective Senior Constable Gaut had sent out countrywide, appealing for anyone who may know of a schoolgirl born around the same time as Tegan Lane, with a similar name or a connection to a person with the surname Norris, to supply the detective with the relevant information. If you are a school who hasn't replied, please hurry up in doing so, was the message from the Coroner. The investigation couldn't be completed until all the questionnaires were in.

Feeling it was imperative too that police be given ample time to follow up on any new leads fresh information may provide them with, Coroner Abernethy glanced at the diary before him and named the date the inquiry would resume. There was a stunned silence in the court while everyone tried to take on board what had just happened. And then loud whisperings as the relevance of the date dawned on the assembled courtroom: the new date was September 12, which would be Tegan's ninth birthday if she was still alive!

It certainly hadn't escaped an anguished Keli's notice that the case had been adjourned until her daughter's birthday. Add to that the fact that an adjournment meant the painful case dragging on even longer, and the morning's short proceedings became too much for the 30-year-old, who became visibly upset. Distraught she turned to her father and collapsed in to his arms inconsolable. "I know the family want to get the matter over with," continued Coroner Abernethy. "But the greater interest is locating the child and finding out what's happened to her."

As it happened the extra time that the Coroner granted police helped very little and a request was later made for even more time. It wasn't until February 2006 – eight months after Coroner Abernethy had first adjourned Keli taking the stand, and almost ten years since the disappearance of Tegan – that the case was finally resumed. Even then it was decided that Detective Senior Constable Gaut would be called back to the stand to give more evidence on the latest findings to the court, before Keli was questioned.

Detective Senior Constable Gaut was always going to have a tough interrogation from Keli's legal team. Despite his best efforts, even he accepted that the investigation had been botched, and was at best extremely tardy. There was a serious problem with police resources and that in turn led to major delays. It was simply too big a job for the officers involved and by the time many of the trails were followed up, it was too late – they were well and truly cold. Keli's lawyer Mr Hamill blasted the detective for the continual delays in the investigation and particularly the length of time that passed before the first interview with Keli was conducted.

"The truth of the matter," he said, "is that Miss Lane was not interviewed until the year 2001. The whole of the year 2000 went past without a police officer crossing her doorstep or giving her a call. As a competent policeman, would it be about the first thing you did? You might make background checks first before speaking to her, yes, you might do that, but you would certainly interview her some time soon, would you not?"

"I imagine so," replied Detective Senior Constable Gaut. But that wasn't a good enough answer for the lawyer. "Well would you imagine so or are you clear?" he pressed. "Well I wasn't around at that stage so I don't know what the circumstances were at Manly," said Detective Senior Constable Gaut.

Despite police becoming aware in 1999 of a missing baby girl born in 1996, it wasn't until March 2005 that the search began in earnest to find Tegan. It was Mr Hamill's belief that Detective Senior Constable Gaut and his team had instead been caught up in delving into Keli's private life, which was intrinsically linked to locating Tegan's whereabouts. "You do not agree with the proposition I suppose that you became so preoccupied with Ms Lane's private life that you did not really start the serious undertaking [to find the child]?" asked Hamill. "I do disagree with that," replied Detective Senior Constable Gaut.

The investigation had, however, been hindered, Detective Senior Constable Gaut admitted, because he had found it very difficult to believe anything that Keli said. She had already told him a pack of lies and provided authorities with a mass of misinformation. "Plainly, without mincing words, it has caused you to be suspicious of her," said Mr Hamill. "That's correct," said Detective Senior Constable Gaut.

Mr Hamill believed that from the very beginning the police had conducted their inquiries with a preconceived idea that Keli was guilty of something and that she was a suspect in a possible death. "In 2004, I think January, again you didn't tell her she was a suspect, did you?" he asked.

"I'd actually asked her in the interview prior if she'd killed her child, so I think it was clear in Keli's mind that I was looking at all avenues." Detective Senior Constable Gaut said that to him Keli's story sounded illogical and he felt she knew more than she was telling police. "From this point onwards," he said, "the only evidence of Tegan being alive and well comes from Keli Lane."

Mr Hamill didn't believe that every word Keli Lane had uttered to police was a lie. He referred to the videotaped interview from 2003, conducted by Detective Senior Constable Gaut, which lasted 85

Even an experienced police officer was baffled. "It's one of the strange ones," the detective said in court. "I didn't know if it was a truthful reaction or nor to be honest."

minutes. Despite Keli's constant insistence that ex-boyfriend Duncan Gillies wasn't involved in Tegan's disappearance, police still hadn't believed her. Mr Hamill told the court that the look of shock on Keli's face when police suggested they believed Duncan was the father, was a genuine look that couldn't be faked.

"Her response was a very strong and emotional one?" Mr Hamill asked. "That's correct," Detective Senior Constable Gaut replied. "And her reaction to it was from looking at [it with your] police instincts, was that her reaction was a truthful one and it was one of the strongest responses she had in the course of that interview?" he continued. "Yeah, that's true," said the detective. "It's one of the strange ones. I didn't know if it was a truthful reaction or not to be honest."

Keli's legal team was intent on proving that what she had said about the whereabouts of Tegan was the truth. A good way to achieve this was to test her claim that she had driven herself home from Auburn Hospital on the day she discharged herself – two days after Tegan's birth – and that she then arrived at a Manly wedding, all within two hours. On the advice from Keli's solicitor, Mary Bova – who prepared much of Keli's case for the coronial inquest and then brought in lawyer Peter Hamill to represent Keli – on Saturday June 18, 2005, Keli's father Robert Lane did a test drive.

Robert Lane hopped behind the wheel of his vehicle in the driveway of the family's Fairlight home at 12:30pm, then took the most direct route to Auburn Hospital. He travelled along Military Road, through the northern Sydney suburb of Crows Nest, down Victoria and Silverwater Roads to his destination. As he pulled up in the car park he looked at his watch, which read 1:40pm – it had taken him exactly one hour and 10 minutes. He then turned around and drove home to Fairlight, but this time he went via Venus Street, Gladesville where Keli had – in one of her versions – claimed to have stopped off (that being the address where she spent half her time living with boyfriend Duncan Gillies). In total that trip took one hour and six minutes. If Keli had left Auburn Hospital at 2pm, driven home, quickly changed into a dressy outfit and arrived at a Manly wedding two hours later, then she would indeed have had very little time to do anything with Tegan other than hand her over to her father, Andrew Norris, in the hospital car park, as she had claimed.

Police, though, were keeping all of their options open. Indeed, some of the potential scenarios that could have taken place were not particularly pleasant. Keli's drive home that day had taken her past Lane Cove National Park – a vast expanse of bushland in Sydney's north – and shocking as it was to even imagine, she could easily have dumped her newborn baby in the bushland, knowing there was very little chance her body would ever be found. And if three years were to pass, the likelihood of discovering any remains at all was remote.

The other possibility, less grisly, but just as distressing, was whether Keli Lane could have had time to sell her baby and hand her over, and still make the Manly wedding by 4pm?

Both scenarios were mere speculation, but without concrete evidence backing up anything Keli had claimed to be the truth, police, press and public couldn't help but picture other possible outcomes to the mystery.

The only certainty seemed to be that as more time passed, the police became more and more sceptical of Keli's claim that her baby, Tegan

Lee Lane, was with her natural father. But Mr Hamill was insistent that Robert Lane's test drive supported Keli's claims, because the crucial timing of her journeys accounted for her story as to her movements that day.

Mr Hamill didn't like the way the police had handled the investigation and believed they had resorted to bullying potential witnesses to force them to sign statements, a claim made by Keli's close friends Brandon and Melinda Ward. "Did you say to Brandon Ward – look the people that don't give a statement are going to be called to court?" Hamill asked. "No, I didn't say that," Detective Senior Constable Gaut replied.

At that moment Coroner Abernethy interrupted Keli's lawyer to support the police officer. "Well, that is a fair thing to say anyway, I think that is what usually happens … [to] tell them if they do not give a statement we have got no option and that is a normal thing, that is not bullying."

Knowing the inquiry was rapidly coming to a close, the press bench had asked court staff – ahead of time – if they could have printed copies of Coroner Abernethy's findings when he handed them down (read them to the court). But he was swift and curt in his reply – no, if the media wanted to quote what he said, they would have to write quickly! (The findings of a coroner, when he/she announces them at the end of an inquiry, can be lengthy and dense in detail; containing many names, dates and critical legal information, which it is vital for a reporter to write down correctly. Even for a veteran court reporter, taking these final findings down can be testing on the fastest of shorthand.) Abernethy would not provide them with a transcript: "I told the press to sharpen their pencils," he said. "My word I did."

Coroner Abernethy's refusal to supply reporters with a copy of the statement he would read from rather summed up his relationship with the media throughout, not only in the Tegan Lane case but during his many years serving as a coroner. John Abernethy disliked the press pack.

Throughout the 2005 coronial inquest into the disappearance of Tegan Lane, the media had requested access to photographs (such as of Keli back in 1996) that were tendered to the court, and also to the recorded police interviews with Keli and other witnesses. The press were well within their legal rights and in most cases it is not a problem (as anything read or presented in an open court is for public knowledge and can be accessed by the media, unless the judge or coroner believes there are exceptional circumstances, in which case a suppression order is normally put in place). But Coroner Abernethy blocked access wherever possible, "I am not going to let the media have a look at anything," he said at the very beginning of the inquest on June 20, 2005.

It developed into a stoush of sorts. John Fairfax and Sons, Nationwide News and TCN Channel Nine jointly hired a barrister to argue for the release of particular documents, so that once they were tendered to the court, they could become public record. The chief request was for the videotape of the formal interviews police had conducted with Keli, and for a transcript of Detective Senior Constable Gaut's statement (the one presented to the court when he gave his evidence).

"There's an ongoing investigation," Coroner Abernethy rasped, "into the disappearance of a child. One of the things I have to keep in the back of my mind, and I hate to have to say this in front of the Lane family and others, but you forced the issue, is whether or not this child has been done away with. In those circumstances the media's need to look at that sort of thing goes right back to nothing … we are dealing with a matter that is still unresolved. The answer is no."

The media companies' lawyer, Matthew Richardson, was not deterred by Coroner Abernethy's outburst though, and he pressed on, saying he had further submissions to make to the court and kindly wished to outline them. "You can make them in writing," barked Abernethy, "and present them tomorrow morning, but I am not going to grant that. The media comes firmly second to the interests of this court in establishing whether or not this child is alive or dead, and the possibility that they use these things in the future. No. No. Go away!"

When the case resumed the following morning, Coroner Abernethy appeared to have had a change of heart, albeit not of his own will.

"It seems I do not have much choice," he told the court, explaining that legally, the media had every right to access the exhibits. "I can predict with a reasonable degree of certainty," he quipped, "what will happen when these videos are reproduced – we will have the most salacious snippets."

Keli Lane's lawyer Peter Hamill had criticism of the actions of the press too. He believed the waiting media had hounded his client when she arrived and left court each day. "I think in one sense my client was probably subjected to a technical assault as she attempted to get away from the court," he said.

"Yes, I noticed the footage and again I have to say one of the [media] agencies acted disgracefully in front of this courthouse and I for the life of me cannot understand why," replied Coroner Abernethy, adding that despite repeated requests from his staff the day before not to film the Coroner as he left the building, some members of the press had ignored that request and still done so.

"I am broad shouldered about it," he went on. "I have been in the game too long. I have been on this bench for 21 years and frankly nothing surprises me or bothers me now.

"But I do feel for the people who come to my court and leave the court and are subjected to this disgraceful behaviour, being followed, harangued accosted by the press in the interests of a story... It is just humbug, frankly the behaviour of the press in the electronic media in certain cases that I have been involved in. I do not have to talk about ones I have not been involved with but I have got a pair of eyes and I can see what happens in other cases."

Coroner Abernethy then mentioned the media's behaviour during the 2004 inquest into the death of Aboriginal teenager TJ Hickey. It was a controversial case and Coroner Abernethy was angry at the media's treatment of the teenager's family and friends. The 17-year-old died in February 2004 when he was impaled on a fence after coming off his bicycle. The accident happened in the crime-riddled inner Sydney suburb of Redfern. There were claims that TJ was being chased by police at the time of his death and immediately that caused outrage within the Aboriginal community, which led to the notorious Redfern riots, one of the worst street fights in the city's history.

The inquest into his death was highly charged and Coroner Abernethy, it seemed, certainly believed the media aggravated an already volatile situation.

"I am not tarring the media, I am tarring a few photographers with their big heavy cameras, jostling and pushing. It is not a rugby field. We should not be chasing people like that. It is daunting enough to come to this plac e– the added stressor is the press. The press is a necessary evil and Miss Lane was not born yesterday, she knows that and accepts that. Ms Lane is entitled to a little of privacy. Sure she can be photographed, but these close-ups and jostling her and jostling the people with her, her father and husband …

"I do not really feel like granting your application [the media's request for access to photographs tendered to the court during the

The coroner criticised the jostling by the media. "It is not a rugby field," he said. "We should not be chasing people like that. It is daunting enough to come to this place."

inquiry and videotaped police interviews with Keli], although as Mr Hamill concedes and I concede, the law seems to be that we should give them up to you."

The three recorded formal interviews with Keli Lane ran for several hours and at particular points she became quite distressed and anxious. It was for that reason that Coroner Abernethy wanted to know exactly which segments of the tape the television reporters would air. Media lawyer Mr Matthew Richardson pointed out to the Coroner that the journalists were well aware of defamation and contempt laws, and if Keli felt she had been in any way treated unfairly, she had the avenue available to her to take court action. (A reporter faces the possibility of being fined or sent to prison if they make a false accusation or maliciously misrepresent someone. The court takes such matters very seriously and all court reporters are mindful of this when writing their reports.)

"Yes and how much does it cost to sue?" Coroner Abernethy continued. "How can she possibly go and sue a media mogul for defamation? I mean it does not happen. Those who are well-heeled, fair enough, but no one is suggesting Ms Lane is the richest woman in Australia. She is not."

But finally the Coroner agreed to hand over the transcript of the police interview to the journalists during the lunch break. He wanted them to highlight the paragraphs they planned to run on the news. Thankfully, when Coroner Abernethy looked at the paragraphs pinpointed by the reporters, he was happy and satisfied that they had no plans to take what Keli had said out of context.

Whatever the Coroner may have thought, the journalists who had trooped to the inquiry each day were not out to paint a picture of Keli as some sort of monster. Rather, we were just as intrigued and puzzled by the case as the police and the public and wanted Tegan Lee Lane to be found alive and healthy just as much as everyone else.

In the end, press treatment of Keli Lane aside, she wasn't called to give evidence on Tegan's ninth birthday – September 12, 2005 – after all. Instead Keli Lane and her family spent another Christmas with the scandal of "missing" Tegan Lane hanging over their heads. And until Coroner John Abernethy made his ruling as to what he believed had happened to Tegan, it was impossible for any of them to even think about moving on or trying to get on with their lives.

Normally as a court reporter I would cover the opening and closing days of a trial and inquest and only turn up otherwise if I knew an interesting or crucial witness would be giving evidence.

That wasn't the case with the Tegan Lane inquest. Every witness was vital and could be the key to determining what happened to her. I neglected all other cases during that time.

Each day I would make the hour's drive to Westmead Coroner's Court to hear the latest developments in the case, and every day I would be hoping it would be the day when we finally got somewhere – a breakthrough!

When the case was suddenly adjourned I was left with an empty feeling inside and I had to turn my mind to what other cases were unfolding in Sydney. Unfortunately you can always find them!

It was the year of Tegan Lee Lane's 10th birthday when the word finally came through that Keli Lane would take the stand – on February 14, 2006. Valentine's Day.

This time when Keli Lane arrived at Westmead Coroner's Court, ready to take the stand, there was less fuss from the media, less jostling and pushing. Maybe the press had heeded Coroner Abernethy's warning, or maybe they had all seen one too many false starts in this case and had fewer expectations about what they were about to witness.

Again Keli was accompanied only by her father, Robert Lane – no sign of her mother Sandra, her brother Morgan or her husband. When her name was called to come forward, she walked to the front of the courtroom stiffly and sat with her hands folded. She listened patiently as the court officer read her the oath, which Keli had to repeat, her hand on *The Bible*.

Then Sergeant Becroft began by asking the most obvious and direct question first. "Can you tell this court what happened to Tegan Lane around 2pm on September 14, 1996, when you left the hospital with her?" she asked.

At that moment everyone in the courtroom was holding their breath. Despite mobile phones being banned from the courtroom, every journalist had their phone "on silent" ready to send a text message back to their newsroom to report Keli's long-awaited response.

Shifting slightly in her chair, Keli Lane, the woman who had been caught up in the media headlights for so long, who every reporter would have dropped their biggest story to interview, leaned forward closer to the microphone, looked directly at the Coroner and said in a strong, but soft voice: "I do not wish to answer that question!"

(My text to my Channel Nine newsroom: *Keli refuses to answer, damn!*)

With those eight short words, the coronial inquest into the disappearance of Tegan Lane – which had dragged on for 15 months – was over. Despite an exhaustive search and extensive interviews by police, neither Andrew Norris – whom Keli claimed was Tegan's real father – nor Tegan herself had been found.

There was no one in that room who looked more pricked with disappointment than the Coroner himself.

Keli's lawyer Peter Hamill then stood up and said that he had instructed his client not to give evidence on the basis that it might incriminate her.

"It's self-evident," he said, "my client is a suspect in what is likely to be an ongoing search for a missing person or persons in an ongoing investigation." He said Ms Lane was well within her rights to refuse to answer and that she was entitled to exercise her right to silence. "I have great concerns," he continued "that any evidence she gives in these proceedings could be used against her in future proceedings."

With Keli's refusal to assist police any further with their inquiries by answering any more questions, all that was left was for the coroner's assisting counsel, Sergeant Rebbecca Becroft, and Keli's lawyer, Mr Peter Hamill, to make their final submissions to the court. Coroner John Abernethy would consider what had been put before him before giving his final ruling.

In summing up the evidence for the police, the assisting counsel, Sergeant Becroft, told the Coroner that Ms Lane had "told a number of half-truths and untruths to the investigating officers," and that her account of what happened "seems unbelievable." She believed there could be only three possible scenarios as to what happened to Tegan Lane: she was with her natural father, she had been given to a person unknown, or she had met with foul play.

While the purpose of the inquest was to determine whether Tegan was alive or dead, Sergeant Becroft accepted, that on the evidence provided, the Coroner could not be satisfied that Ms Lane had committed an indictable offence (a serious criminal offence which entitles the defendant to a trial by jury) although clearly Coroner Abernethy would be the judge of that.

She said it could not be ruled out that Tegan was alive and living under a false name with her biological father.

"This case can be described using a number of adjectives," she said, "bizarre, fascinating, unusual, unbelievable. However, at the end of the day, what happened to … Tegan Lane is a question that still has no definitive answer."

In his closing address to the Coroner, Mr Hamill said: "The emotion and confusion displayed in her interviews with police is entirely consistent with a young woman whose deepest secrets are in the process of unravelling and being disclosed to the closest people in her life – people from whom she had, remarkably, been able to keep them." He accepted that she had "spun an extraordinary web of deceit" but denied that she had done anything wrong.

Keli Lane's actions, said Mr Hamill, were those of a woman who was embarrassed about her sexual conduct and her failure to adequately protect herself against pregnancy. He was emphatic in his belief that she didn't fit the profile of a "desperate mother" who killed her baby and then denied any knowledge of the pregnancy. Rather, he believed that Keli had relinquished the child to a person in a better position to care for her, that person being Tegan's father.

Mr Hamill strongly believed that Keli's lies were consistent with a person who was trying to keep all of her pregnancies secret from the people in her life. "The fact is that the lies and secrecy and misinformation and deceit apply equally throughout all of the pregnancies." He pointed out that in 1996, when Tegan was born, it was very easy to register a child under another name. (It was because of this inquiry into missing Tegan, and the subsequent recognition of loopholes in the system for registering births in Australia, that new guidelines were put in place.)

"There is no evidence capable of establishing beyond reasonable doubt that Tegan is dead and, therefore, no evidence capable of establishing any form of homicide," said Mr Hamill. "Furthermore, the evidence of Keli Lane's impeccable character and qualities, and her love of children as well as the history of the three pregnancies – each of which is carried secretly to term and followed by a brief period of breastfeeding and bonding, followed by a complete separation from the child – is utterly at odds with any form of homicide."

There was no doubt that the case had had an enormous effect on Keli Lane's mental state. "The emotionally charged nature of these proceedings," said Mr Hamill "makes speculation inevitable but extremely dangerous and hurtful."

Armed with summings up from both Keli's lawyer and Sergeant Becroft, Coroner Abernethy decided that he needed a little time to consider his position, before making a ruling.

He adjourned the inquiry one last time – until two o'clock the following afternoon. Accepting that Keli had told a litany of lies, he said he had to consider the very real possibility that Tegan had been "done away with."

As the journalists, lawyers and police officers packed their bags at Westmead Coroner's Office that day, there was a feeling at last of the finality of the proceedings. Friendships struck up between professionals over the past 15 months would soon be broken off, as we went our separate ways – onto new cases, new stories, off to new locations. Meanwhile would the dust settle on the document boxes marked *Tegan Lane*?

For Coroner John Abernethy, there was perhaps a sleepless night as he made his mind up on what had become an unenviable case to rule. With the scant evidence available to him, what was the right decision to come to, indeed was there one at all?

But as we all trooped out of the courthouse, what was Keli Lane thinking? Would she finally be able to get on with her life, resume the life she had once – a long time ago? Or would tomorrow's verdict mean she would never be able to escape the events of September 12, 1996; the day she gave birth to a baby girl she called Tegan Lee Lane?

a frustrated coroner

~~THE SEARCH MUST GO ON~~

chapter **11**

MORE THAN 20 years on the job as a coroner investigating suspicious deaths and strange disappearances, but few inquiries had got to John Abernethy – the coroner investigating the case of missing Tegan Lane – like this one did.

One of his last cases before he was due to retire, Coroner Abernethy appeared at times as though the frustration of not being able to get to the bottom of what had happened to baby Tegan, was eating away at him. Perhaps it was because he was nearing retirement that this disappearance affected him so much. Or maybe it was because his normal workload involved the disappearance or death of an adult, rather than a defenceless young child.

Whatever, and it may well have been both, Coroner Abernethy wanted the last few cases brought before him to reach the perfect conclusion, and because he had watched countless innocent children suffer as they were let down by adults who failed to protect them, he was especially frustrated and baffled by this case.

And it wasn't just the mystery of what had happened to baby Tegan that bothered him – although of course it was foremost on his mind. There were also two other children Keli Lane had given birth to, although the case had not centred much on their identity (and we were not allowed to identify them) and their parentage. It was still to be determined who had fathered them.

A DNA test had ruled out Keli's boyfriend of four years from 1994 until 1998, rugby union player Duncan Gillies, as being the father of the first born baby girl in 1995. He was overseas when the third child, a son born in 1999 was conceived, and since there has been no sign of baby Tegan it is impossible to know whether he in fact fathered the little girl. So who on earth was the man responsible for these pregnancies, and did the same one man father all three, or did they all have different fathers? Three children and no idea who their fathers were.

As the Coroner, Abernethy's first task was to determine whether he believed that Tegan was deceased. If he couldn't do so, he had two options: either to make a finding that she was in fact alive and terminate the inquest pursuant to Section 21, Coroners Act 1980, or, as Keli's lawyer Mr Hamill had suggested, he could return an open finding as to death.

If he went for the first option, that he felt satisfied that she was dead, he must then determine when and where she died, and the manner and cause of her death. In cases such as this one, where no body has been located, he must be "comfortably satisfied" as to the fact of death. From there it is a balance of probabilities as to date, place, manner and cause of death.

As the Coroner, Abernethy's first task was to determine whether he believed that Tegan was deceased ... depending on this finding would be a number of consequences.

In handing down his findings on February 15, 2006, Coroner Abernethy explained he had one other obligation. "If satisfied to the required standard of death, I must consider the *admissible* evidence [evidence that a trial judge or jury may consider because the rules of evidence deem it reliable] before me in order to forecast whether or not a reasonable jury, properly instructed, might find that a known person has committed an indictable offence in relation to the death of Tegan Lane. If so satisfied I must terminate this inquest and forward the papers to the Director of Public Prosecutions with the name of the known person and the particulars of the offence committed."

What that meant is whether or not he felt there was enough "reliable" evidence to charge Keli Lane with the death of Tegan, he had to consider whether he thought there was a reasonable chance that a jury of 12 people – if that same evidence was put in front of them – would convict her. If Coroner Abernethy felt that was the case and that they would, he would then make a recommendation to the DPP that Keli should be charged.

Coroner Abernethy agreed with both Keli's lawyer Mr Hamill and Sergeant Becroft, that there was insufficient admissible evidence available to pass the case to the DPP and consider laying criminal charges against Keli Lane. He felt – as had been put to him by Mr Hamill in his closing argument – that the police search for Tegan had not been exhaustive, and so for that, and other reasons, he found it difficult to rule that Tegan was deceased. However, he conceded that in a case such as this, it would be difficult to imagine that any search could ever be exhausted.

In coming to his decision, Coroner Abernethy had before him a large brief of evidence, gathered by Detective Senior Constable Gaut, with the assistance of the Coroner's Investigation Team, and the NSW Police Homicide Squad.

This is what he knew as a fact, for sure: that Tegan Lee Lane had been born on September 12, 1996, at Auburn Hospital to Keli Lane. "Her whereabouts, indeed, whether or not she is in fact alive have not been established since she was discharged from the hospital into the care of her mother Keli on September 14, 1996," he said. "In my view there is clear evidence of the birth of Tegan Lane and at one stage I suggested that the Principal Registrar of Births, Deaths and Marriages register the birth. That has now been attended to."

One of the key focuses for Coroner Abernethy was the two-hour time frame during which Keli left Auburn Hospital and arrived at the Manly wedding of friends with then boyfriend Duncan Gillies. "I think it is pertinent to explain that Auburn Hospital is in the central western suburbs of Sydney, near Parramatta, whereas Manly is on the Warringah Peninsular, a drive at that time of perhaps one hour or a little more. The drive would normally take one through the congested lower north shore of Sydney. On Keli's final version she went via Gladesville where she actually stopped. Tegan Lane's whereabouts cannot be established since her discharge from hospital with her mother. This birth too was kept secret from family and friends and never registered."

For Mr Abernethy, the decision by Keli not to give evidence did not come as a surprise – that was what he had expected – but it still came as a let-down, since Keli was the main link to determining what had happened to Tegan. "Keli Lane has given varying accounts to the DoCS officers, adoption agency social workers and investigating police. She has told untruths to many people about what she did with the child, the identity of the father and where the child is, or might be, now."

Before reaching his conclusion, Mr Abernethy read to the court his account of what had taken place during the inquest. It was his view that the matter "did not come to the attention of NSW Police in a vacuum as it were."

He believed that the DoCS played a leading role in the investigation – indeed it was an alert child protection officer, John Borovnik, from the Katoomba office, whose vigilance caused him to stumble upon evidence of Keli Lane's previous two pregnancies. It was through his inquiries, particularly those with Anglicare social worker Virginia Fung, that he discovered that Ms Lane had provided a false residential address – that being 70 Venus Street, Gladesville – when in fact no such address existed. It was, however, the same street that Duncan Gillies lived on, but there was no number 70. On noting that Keli Lane gave the name Julie Melville as her midwife to staff at Auburn Hospital, Mr Borovnik dug further, only to find that there was no registered midwife by that name. Calls to the NSW Nurses Registration Board found that Ms Melville was a registered nurse, who also happened to be Duncan Gillies mother.

"It was armed with as much data as he could obtain, Borovnik finally telephoned Keli Lane," wrote Coroner Abernethy in his report. "Not satisfied, the police were notified. Initially the investigation was headed by Detective Senior Constable Kehoe, who made a number of his own inquires. However it wasn't until 15 months later that Keli was called into the station for a formal recorded interview.

"A substantial time elapsed before Keli Lane was first interviewed by Kehoe and the matter lay in abeyance for another substantial period of time."

Here the Coroner was focusing on the lengthy delays in the investigation. It was November 7, 1999 when Manly police were first alerted to the disappearance of Tegan Lane, yet they did not call Keli Lane in for an interview until February 14, 2001.

When, in May of that year, Detective Senior Constable Kehoe was transferred to another station, the case lay dormant, until it was handed to Detective Senior Constable Gaut to pick up, on October 9, 2002 – more than a year later.

"The present investigation under Detective Senior Constable Gaut has been thorough. It has always been problematic, though. Firstly, the length of time that had elapsed before Gaut himself became involved made the discovery increasingly difficult. Secondly, Kehoe himself was hardly timely in relation to the quite substantial inquiries he did make. I am certainly not blaming the current officer-in-charge, nor for that matter am I blaming Detective Senior Constable Kehoe. I am however criticising the police system. The investigation was always a serious one and if there were resource problems these officers should have been resourced so that they could get on with the job of locating the child. I am far from satisfied that any senior officer at Manly had any input at all into the matter, or took any meaningful responsibility for ensuring that there was a timely and efficient investigation into it."

Coroner Abernethy recognised that Detective Senior Constable Gaut's investigation had been lengthy and time-consuming. It was made especially difficult because he was trying to prove a negative, which was that Tegan Lane was *not* deceased. He also had to deal with a number of inconsistencies in Keli's story. There was the mix-up with the natural father's name, and whether or not she had said Norris or Morris (Keli has always maintained that she told Detective Senior Constable Kehoe "Norris", not "Morris", as is recorded on the official police transcript from her first recorded interview in 2001).

She also claimed that once Andrew Norris, his partner Mel and his mother took custody of Tegan outside Auburn Hospital, she caught a taxi home - despite initially telling Detective Senior Constable Kehoe that Andrew drove her home. Her reasoning for that untruth was that she was embarrassed to admit that Andrew Norris hated her so much he wouldn't give her a lift. There was also the story that she had driven herself home, but because of the time lapse the decision was made not to forensically examine her car.

The Coroner accepted that Detective Senior Constable Gaut's task was an incredibly difficult one. He had to rely upon the information supplied by Keli to follow up leads, which proved to be impossible since he could never tell if what he was being told was the truth or lies. Besides relying on Keli's account of what had happened, the vigilant detective also used the traditional "strict search and inquiry" method, which was to double check the provided information with the actual evidence or with relevant organisations – that is, a motor vehicle, driver licence, The University of Sydney, the Health Insurance Commission, the mortuary and electoral roles. But that pedestrian search got Detective Senior Constable Gaut nowhere. The Coroner praised his efforts in using a cadaver dog to search the Gladesville home formerly owned by Mr Gillies. The decision to do so was based on Keli's story that she had stopped at Gillies' home on her way to her parents' property at Fairlight. The dog, though, found no trace of Tegan or any remains.

Coroner Abernethy accepted the evidence of Keli's friend and fellow PE student Lisa Andreatta, who Keli had claimed could verify the affair with Norris and that he was Tegan's father and had taken custody of her. When eventually tracked down by police Ms Andreatta denied any knowledge of Andrew Norris, his girlfriend Mel and the birth of Tegan. "I have absolutely no reason not to accept her evidence," said the Coroner.

There were so many lies to unravel: conflicting accounts of what happened when Keli and baby Tegan left Auburn Hospital, and who had turned up to take custody of the child. What Coroner Abernethy couldn't understand was why Keli told Auburn Hospital social worker Ms Baltra-Vasquez untruths about her background and why she claimed to have no support network.

"A very important question asked was, why if she was expecting Norris to attend the hospital, would she lie to the social worker about having no support persons in Sydney. She gave no direct or logical answer to this question," he remarked. "If she was intending to hand the child over at the hospital, why lie to a social worker about supports? She was, after all, handing the child over to its natural father."

Poring over the transcripts of the three formal police interviews Keli participated in, Coroner Abernethy pronounced: "On a fair reading I found many of her answers to sensitive questions to be evasive."

During all his years serving as the state's top coroner, no previous case before him had proven to be so frustrating and complex.

The only person who could explain what happened to Tegan – her mother Keli Lane – refused to talk, which left him in a difficult situation.

It was with that knowledge that he read his conclusion to the court.

"It is important to get this matter into perspective. It is fair to say that my jurisdiction readily hears cases involving so-called 'missing persons'. They are, however, almost always missing adults or older juveniles. These are people who can walk and talk, who can form friendships and acquaintanceships, who can become involved in poor relationships and get themselves into trouble.

"The case of a missing infant is rare indeed. It hardly needs to be stated that Tegan Lane is a special class of missing person. She, of course, had none of the abilities I have referred to above."

As the Coroner read his report, Keli Lane – looking pale and drawn – held her father's hand tightly. Not once did she turn her head to look at the packed courtroom.

As the Coroner read his report, Keli – looking pale and drawn – held her father's hand tightly. Neither of them moved as Coroner Abernethy ran through the case. He criticised Ms Lane for the lies she had told and remonstrated with police for the way certain aspects of the investigation were handled. Not once did Keli turn her head to look at the packed courtroom as the findings were read out. The room was mostly filled with journalists who had covered the case from the start, and who were frantically writing notes in shorthand, taking down everything Coroner Abernethy said word for word. This was easily one of the biggest stories of the year, and certainly a courtroom drama that rivaled the Lindy Chamberlain case for intrigue.

Now Coroner Abernethy turned his attention to the term "comfortable belief" – the term used to describe how he felt about the question as to whether Tegan was alive or deceased.

"I am prepared to accept as a starting point, Mr Hamill's submission that the version finally given, despite the litany of untruths and half-truths to various people including NSW Police, is plausible, largely, but not only because here, on this version, for once there was a person,

Andrew Norris, who was prepared unconditionally to take the child, thus saving Keli Lane from the bothersome adoption process where she might have to lie again. He was after all, on her version, the father of the child and adoption was simply not necessary. He could, after all, simply be added to the birth details if that was considered prudent. However Keli has continued to tell a series of untruths in relation to this version. Why?"

It was a very good question, and one that perhaps would never be answered. But Coroner Abernethy tried to address it one last time on this final day in court.

He was keen to relive every aspect of the case before making his final determination – to retrace Keli's movements the day baby Tegan went missing, examine the varying versions regarding how she got home, how many times – if at all – she saw Tegan after she handed her over.

Originally she told police that she saw Tegan on a number of occasions, but later changed her story saying that she only saw her daughter once. There was also the conflicting account she told about a couple who had befriended her and took Tegan to Perth. Later Keli would claim that couple was in fact Andrew Norris and his partner.

"I have to say I find it inherently unlikely that a man with whom she was having an affair, who already had a partner, who initially at least was incredibly angry on learning she was pregnant, nevertheless was happy to take the child. This is all the more unlikely because that man's cuckolded partner also agreed. Finally, Keli Lane added Tegan Lane's name to her own Medicare card whilst at the hospital. No arrangement was ever made to alter that so that Norris could take care of claiming Medicare benefits later on."

Weighing up all the evidence before him, the Coroner's chief task at the end of the day was to make one finding: did he determine that Keli Lane's baby Tegan was alive or dead?

First Coroner Abernethy addressed the possibility that Tegan Lee Lane was alive.

"There are factors going to the proposition that Tegan Lane is alive. They include the final version of events by Keli Lane; the fact that there is no forensic evidence of death; the fact that she entered the adoption process with both the first and third child; the possibility that

Tegan is living under an assumed identity (though that is contingent on acceptance of the Keli Lane version); reticence on the part of those who have her (the family who has Tegan) coming forward."

Next he embarked on the possibility that Tegan was dead. "There are also the pointers to Tegan Lane not being alive. These include the fact that Tegan Lane has not been seen since she was in Auburn Hospital just after birth; the multiplicity of versions and untruths given to a range of persons; the initial denial of giving birth to the child at all; the fact that there has been a very careful search at least in this state of birth records and no sign of the birth being registered; the publicity surrounding 'Andrew Norris and Mel' and the efforts police have made to locate him; the school inquiries; the intense media coverage of this matter from the time Keli Lane was teaching at Ravenswood School."

In the end Coroner Abernethy decided he could not find any truth in the final story Keli spun to police – that baby Tegan was alive and well and living with Andrew Norris, her natural father. "I am completely unable to accept the final version given by Keli Lane," he read.

On hearing the Coroner make that announcement, Keli Lane looked ready to lose control – her shoulders slumped and she started shaking slightly, and had to be comforted by her father.

Still the coroner pressed on.

For the journalists in the room, it was difficult at this point to determine which way Abernethy would lean – alive or dead? For the duration of the inquest, the reporters had been discussing between themselves how much, if any, of Keli's story could be believed. Most of us agreed with the Coroner that Keli had based her story on lies, but that didn't necessarily prove or suggest that Tegan was dead.

The Coroner was nearing his decision.

"It is common ground that the untruths as to what happened to Tegan Lane have been told. Whilst I acknowledge her right against self-incrimination, the position is that without Keli Lane's evidence this court is unable to make a final meaningful assessment as to whether this inherently unlikely version of events may be true."

And then he said it. Finally the moment we had all been waiting for. It was time for his decision. With no fuss – he read it out loud, directly, for the record.

"I am comfortably satisfied that Tegan Lane is in fact deceased."

WE LISTENED as Keli Lane let out a loud uncontrollable sob, watched as she broke down in her father's arms. Undoubtedly, until that moment in time, she had been praying that the Coroner would find there was insufficient evidence to determine whether Tegan was alive or dead.

The courtroom was by now in a quiet frenzy.

But the Coroner wasn't finished yet. He had yet to outline his recommendations – as is the practice with all coronial inquests. Even though the proceedings were still not finished, journalists defied the court rules – which outlawed the use of mobile phones – and frantically sent text messages to their chiefs-of-staff back at their newsroom, to alert them of the findings.

Coroner Abernethy was far from through, though. This was one of his last inquests before retirement and he had a point he wanted and intended to make. He was feeling too downhearted that the authorities were no closer to learning the whereabouts of Tegan, or what happened to her.

"I have indicated that there is no case against a known person for the homicide of Tegan Lane. I have indicated that there is a possibility that Tegan Lane is alive. Put another way, I could not, on the evidence be satisfied beyond reasonable doubt of Tegan Lane's death. If I am wrong in my finding, and Tegan is located alive and well, it will of course be reversed.

"In the meantime I am disturbed at the possibility that Tegan may have met with foul play. Because of the nature of this particular investigation and the inadequacies of the initial investigation, I am ordering a Brief of Evidence and Transcript of these proceedings be forwarded to the NSW Homicide Squad for assessment and if necessary a re-investigation or further investigation, I ask that any assessment be carried out by a senior criminal investigator, or former criminal investigator with homicide experience."

The Coroner believed that Tegan Lane had died sometime in 1996, probably in the immediate days after her birth. As to the place, manner and cause of the death he was unable to say.

For all those involved it was a disappointing end to a case that had deeply affected their lives. Assisting counsel Sergeant Rebbecca Becroft had dedicated thousands of hours to the inquiry and it wasn't a case that you could simply switch off from at night. It had affected her relationship and her children, as they too lived and breathed the case. Each of them felt the pain and disappointment that the mystery had not been resolved. The same went for Detective Senior Constable Gaut who was gutted by the result, so much so that he felt unable to face the waiting media on that final day. Instead, he slipped out of the back door, which is normally reserved for court staff only.

Everyone who had been involved in the coronial inquest into what happened to baby Tegan Lee Lane had gone through the Westmead Coroner's Court doors each day not knowing the truth, but deep in their hearts – the media included – hoping that somehow the process would shed light on the mystery, and the truth would be revealed. Years of hard work, late nights, sleepless nights … But in this moment it felt as though it had all been for nothing.

What did come of the process, though, was a number of positive recommendations by the Coroner, in regard to what would happen now with this investigation, and how similar investigations could be better handled in the future. A key problem highlighted in the inquest was how easy it was for a birth not to be registered, and for a newborn to go missing, and for that not to be noticed in the system for years, if ever. If Keli Lane hadn't adopted out her third child, then there was a very good chance that the existence of Tegan would never have been known.

The key recommendation made by Coroner Abernethy was for this case to be thoroughly reviewed by the NSW Homicide Squad. It was no longer the case of a missing child, but the suspected death of an infant. Subject to that review was a request for further investigations to take place. The Coroner felt that there were still more avenues to go down in the search for the truth about Tegan, that there was still more work police could do in that area. Most notably he felt that a cross-check of Tegan's birth details with those of others of the same age and sex around the country, was still incomplete – not all schools had responded to Detective Senior Constable Gaut's questionnaire. He also believed that the case should be handled by an experienced senior homicide detective.

The second recommendation was that the NSW Government and the Australian Government take the necessary steps to consider the enactment of a uniform registration code in relation to the registration of births, deaths and marriages throughout all states and territories of Australia.

The reasoning behind this particular recommendation was the recognition that if Tegan was living under an assumed name, there would be very little chance of tracking her down. Had she been registered illegally, under a false name or date of birth, she would be almost impossible to locate. It would have been quite simple for her guardians to vary her birth date slightly, and change her name. The search Detective Senior Constable Gaut had conducted was based on Tegan being registered with the correct birth date. If the date had been varied, say from September 9 to September 11, that would mean the exhaustive checks being carried out by police were always going to come to nothing. The discovery of a Teagan Chapman in Queensland, and the initial belief that she could in fact have been the missing Tegan, was proof of how flawed the process was.

Finally, the Coroner called on the NSW Government to consider the introduction of legislation that would place greater responsibility on hospitals, midwives and other relevant health care workers to report the details of all births to the Registry of Births Deaths and Marriages. That process is now underway, with a bill put to the Parliament of New South Wales in June 2007 ensuring authorities are notified of a birth within seven days.

It felt as though Tegan Lane's birth had not been in vain. It was thanks to her that these changes were made.

But Keli Lane, the woman who still sat in the courtroom, listening as the Coroner made his recommendations for new legislation – trying to make some good come out of so much bad – the woman who still had the power to unlock the mystery, to put all these professionals out of their misery, was clearly paying her own price too. The 15-month inquiry had stripped her of any privacy – and her family too. Now she had to cope with the knowledge that the inquiry was not over either. And all of this was obviously extremely difficult for her to come to terms with.

Her lawyer Peter Hamill and her father Robert Lane both physically helped Keli – both taking hold of her arms and slowly walking her out the side entrance of the courtroom – into one of the interview rooms, where she could sit and try to pull herself together.

Of course, Keli had been hoping the Coroner would believe the final version of events she told police, and would make a finding that Tegan was alive and well and living with her biological father somewhere. News that the case would be forwarded to the Homicide Squad caused her great stress – it meant the nightmare was far from over. It would continue to haunt both her and her family as they struggled to put their lives back together.

A month after the inquest, the NSW Police Commissioner Ken Moroney moved to assemble a team of experienced detectives from the Unsolved Homicide Squad. Their sole task was to crack the Tegan Lane mystery. A spokesperson for the Commissioner told *The Sun-Herald* newspaper on March 5, 2006, that Mr Moroney was keen for investigations to continue. "The commissioner agrees with the recommendations made by the NSW Coroner," the spokesperson said, and he was hoping fresh eyes might uncover further avenues.

For Coroner Abernethy, the case of missing Tegan Lane would indeed be one of his final inquests. Top dog among NSW coroners since January 2000, he had worked as a full-time coroner since 1994, but he was finally hanging up his hat to retire at the age of 59. In his final interview with *The Daily Telegraph's* Kara Lawrence in September 2006 he told her that he loved the job, but often found it confronting.

"I love to solve mysteries," he said. "It is fascinating. That's why I'm in it. To most people, medical examination and crime-scene examination are fascinating. Unsolved murders are fascinating."

He said what troubled him the most, though, were missing and dead babies, and that the Tegan Lane mystery is the case that will continue to frustrate him the most – certainly something coming from a man who had investigated 6,000 unnatural, or "suspected" deaths every year.

"It's just unfortunate," he said. "No matter what lengths we went to, we hit a dead end. We had a real, live mother sitting in court and we just couldn't figure it out."

POSTSCRIPT

THE CLOSING of the coronial inquest was far from the end for 32-year-old Keli Lane. The case still hangs over her head and she is painfully aware that an investigation is currently underway which may uncover yet more deceptions.

The cost, both emotionally and financially, for Keli has been crippling. Massive legal bills have forced her to consider moving back into the family home. The services of Peter Hamill Special Counsel – a well-known and respected barrister – don't come cheap, and when the case dragged on for months and months, as police extended their investigations, the lawyer's bill spiralled out of control.

Struggling to cope financially, Keli has had to take on extra employment. She works as a receptionist for a local chiropractor on the northern beaches, but now also sells swimming lessons at a local shopping mall on behalf of Definition Health Club's Brookvale pool, for extra cash.

Her primary concern, though, is her six-year-old daughter who she drops to school each day on her way to work.

Keli Lane, one-time water-polo champ, has paid a heavy price for her secrets and lies, and her marriage may also have suffered. One of her husband's rugby league-playing friends told *The Sun-Herald* on March 5, 2006: "He has done it very tough over the past two years. He had no idea about any of this when he met her."

Her immediate family has suffered terribly too. The Lanes were well-known, liked and respected in their community and their friends say the scandal has changed them all beyond recognition.

Tragically, it's now rare to see Robert and Sandra Lane out in public. One friend told *The Sun-Herald* on March 5, 2006, that the investigation had taken a particularly heavy toll on Keli's mother Sandra.

"Before this all erupted, you'd bump into Keli's mum almost daily," said the family friend. "She was a very happy, outgoing woman. But Keli's situation still remains a conversation piece. Until the child is found the whole family will remain in limbo."